Constraint Programming Languages

Their Specification and Generation

Wm Leler

235418

ADDISON-WESLEY PUBLISHING COMPANY
Reading, Massachusetts • Menlo Park, California • New York
Don Mills, Ontario • Wokingham, England • Amsterdam • Bonn • Sydney
Singapore • Tokyo • Madrid • Bogotá • Santiago • San Juan

This book is in the Addison-Wesley Series in Computer Science
Michael A. Harrison, Consulting Editor

This document was formatted using Troff and PostScript,
and printed using the following fonts:
New Century Schoolbook
Helvetica
Courier
Symbol

Library of Congress Cataloging-in-Publication Data

Leler, Wm (William)
   Constraint Programming Languages
     Their Specification and Generation
   Bibliography: p.
   Includes index.
   1. Bertrand (Computer program language) I. Title.
QA76.73.B47L45   1988   005.13'3   87-1236
ISBN 0-201-06243-7

Preface

Constraint languages represent a new programming paradigm with applications in such areas as the simulation of physical systems, computer-aided design, VLSI, graphics, and typesetting. Constraint languages are *declarative*; a programmer specifies a desired goal, not a specific algorithm to accomplish that goal. As a result, constraint programs are easy to build and modify, and their nonprocedural nature makes them amenable for execution on parallel processors.

This book is aimed at researchers investigating declarative programming languages and rewrite rule systems, and engineers interested in building useful systems using constraint-satisfaction techniques. It provides an introduction to the subject of constraint satisfaction, a survey of existing systems, and introduces a new technique that makes constraint-satisfaction systems significantly easier to create and extend. A general-purpose specification language called **Bertrand** is defined that allows a user to describe a constraint-satisfaction system using rules. This language uses a new inference mechanism called **augmented term rewriting** to execute the user's specification. Bertrand supports a rule-based programming methodology, and also includes a form of abstract data type. Using rules, a user can describe new objects and new constraint-satisfaction mechanisms. This book shows how existing constraint-satisfaction systems can be implemented using Bertrand, and gives examples of how to use Bertrand to solve algebraic word and computer-aided engineering problems, and problems in graphics involving computer-aided design, illustration, and mapping. It also gives a precise operational semantics for augmented term rewriting, and presents techniques for efficient execution, including interpretation using fast pattern matching, and compilation.

The software described in this document is available for a nominal charge. Inquiries should be directed to the author at the following address:

P.O. Box 69044
Portland, Oregon 97201

Some ideas feel *good* to us. This concept is common enough, although it appeals more to our emotions than our intellect. For example, on the first day of class, the professor of an introductory psychology class I took declared [Nydegger 1973]:

> "It will be my task during this semester to convince you that behaviorism is not only correct, but that it is right and good."

Another example appears in the IDEAL user's manual [Van Wyk 1981]:

> "To take advantage of IDEAL's capabilities, you must believe that *complex numbers are good*."

IDEAL uses complex numbers to represent two-dimensional graphical points, the advantage being that, because all objects in IDEAL are complex numbers, the same operators and functions can be used on all objects, whether they represent numbers or points.

Why do some ideas feel good? Perhaps there is a measure of beauty for ideas, and some are simply more appealing than others. One may worry, however, that a discussion of aesthetic issues is not compatible with the practice of computer science, and that such arguments belong with other questions of taste, such as those about the right way to indent nested loops or the proper choice of variable names. Indeed, one sometimes hears computer scientists making exhortations resembling those of the psychology professor quoted above. A fairly well-known example of this is the so-called war between the "big-endians" and the "little-endians," concerning whether the bits and bytes of a machine word should be numbered starting from the most or the least significant end.

Should we reject aesthetic considerations as contrary to scientific method? Experience has shown otherwise. Proper attention to the goals of aesthetics leads to measurably better designs. As Fred Brooks says, "Good esthetics yield good economics." [Blaauw & Brooks p. 86, 1986].

The pursuit of good design principles transcends aesthetics. To avoid meaningless arguments about taste, we must give some basis for our aesthetic judgments. Toward this end, Blaauw and Brooks outline four principles of good design: *consistency, orthogonality, propriety,* and *generality.* They apply their principles to computer architecture, but similar principles apply to other areas. In designing computer languages, two key principles are *simplicity* and *generality.* For example, we can say that the use of complex numbers in IDEAL is *good* because it is *simpler* than having two separate data types, and because it is more *general* to allow operators to work on both numbers and points. To paraphrase something a professor of mine once told me, if you find a simple solution to one problem and then find that the same solution simultaneously solves several other problems, then you are probably onto something exciting. Working with constraint-satisfaction systems has been, and continues to be, very exciting.

Acknowledgements

I wish to thank Bharat Jayaraman for his persistent help with this work, and Fred Brooks for his early encouragement and support. I am truly grateful to the wonderful people at the Tektronix Computer Research Laboratory, especially Rick LeFaivre, for allowing me to spend so much time writing this book. Alas, no list of acknowledgements is ever complete—I need to thank the several dozen people and places who somehow found out about this research and either requested copies of this book or invited me to give talks. I especially want to thank several people whose careful reading and comments on this book were invaluable during its preparation: David Maier, Mike O'Donnell, and Chris Van Wyk, and all the people who supplied encouragement, especially Scott Danforth, Marta Kallstrom, Larry Morandi and Philip Todd.

Dedication

Finally, I must step back from this work and admit that it is not really important at all. There are special people out there who have dedicated their lives to ideas that not only *might* make a difference, but *must*. I dedicate this book to Robin and John Jeavons, whose work on Intensive Farming techniques has already made a difference to a hungry world, and to other people like them who have the courage to work long and hard for the important ideas they believe in.

Wm Leler

Contents

Chapter 1

Introduction

1.1 Imperative versus Constraint Programming

In current imperative computer languages, such as C or Pascal, a program is a step-by-step procedure. To solve a problem using these languages, the user must manually construct and debug a specific executable algorithm. This style of problem solving has become so pervasive that it is common to confuse algorithm design with problem solving. The effort required to program using imperative languages tends to discourage programming and thus effectively restricts most users to canned application programs.

To use an algorithmic program to solve different but related problems, the programmer must anticipate the different problems to be solved and include explicit decision points in the algorithm. For example, using a syntax similar to C or FORTRAN one might write the statement:

$$C = (F - 32) \times 5/9$$

to compute the Celsius (C) equivalent of a Fahrenheit (F) temperature. To convert Fahrenheit temperatures to Celsius, however, a separate statement would have to be included in the program; namely,

$$F = 32 + 9/5 \times C$$

along with a branch (*if*) statement to choose which statement to execute. To be able to convert temperatures to and from degrees Kelvin, even more statements (with the associated branch points) would have to be added:

$$K = C - 273$$
$$C = K + 273$$
$$K = 290.78 + 5/9 \times F$$
$$F = 523.4 + 9/5 \times K$$

As new variables are added to this program, the number of statements grows exponentially.

In constraint languages, programming is a *declarative* task. The programmer states a set of *relations* between a set of *objects*, and it is the job of the constraint-satisfaction system to find a solution that satisfies these relations. Since the specific steps used to satisfy the constraints are largely up to the discretion of the constraint-satisfaction system, a programmer can solve problems with less regard for the algorithms used than when an imperative language is used. For the growing number of computer users untrained in traditional imperative programming, this can be a significant advantage. For example, constraintlike spread-sheet languages (such as VisiCalc, Lotus 1-2-3, and others) allow users to solve many different financial modeling problems without resorting to programming in the traditional sense.

In a constraint language, the statement

$$C \ = \ (F - 32) \times 5/9$$

is a *program* that defines a relationship between degrees Fahrenheit (F) and degrees Celsius (C). Given either F or C, the other can be computed, so the same program can be used to solve at least two different problems, without any explicit decision points. With a typical constraint-satisfaction system, we could also solve for the temperature where the values in degrees Fahrenheit and Celsius are the same (−40 degrees), and so on. The ability to solve many different problems with the same program, even if they were not anticipated when the program was written, is a key advantage of constraint languages.

Constraint programs also are easy to modify and extend — to add the ability to convert between degrees Kelvin (K) and Celsius (C), only a single additional constraint is required:

$$K \ = \ C \ - \ 273$$

In addition, a typical constraint-satisfaction system can combine these two relationships in order to convert between degrees Kelvin and Fahrenheit, for example, without requiring any additional statements.

A program in a constraint language consists of a set of relations between a set of objects. In our constraint-language program, F and C are the objects, which in this case are numbers, and the constraint $C \ = \ (F - 32) \times 5/9$ is the relationship between these two objects. Given a value for either F or C, the constraint-satisfaction system can use the problem-solving rules of algebra to solve for the other.

1.1.1 Assignment versus Equality

The difference between imperative languages and constraint languages is highlighted by their treatment of equality. Algorithmic languages require two (or more) different operators for equality and assignment. For example, in FORTRAN the relational operator .EQ. returns true or false depending on whether its two arguments are equal, and = is used to assign the value of an expression to a variable, whereas in Pascal = is used as the relational operator and : = for assignment.

1. Introduction

In a constraint language, equality is used only as a relational operator, equivalent to the corresponding operator in conventional languages. An assignment operator is unnecessary in a constraint language; the constraint-satisfaction mechanism "assigns" values to variables by finding values for the variables that make the equality relationships true.

For example, in the constraint-language statement

$$X = 5$$

the equal sign is used as a relational operator (as in mathematics), but to make this statement true the constraint-satisfaction system will give the value 5 to X. Thus the equal sign acts similarly to an assignment operator. Unlike the imperative assignment operator, however, arbitrary expressions can appear as its left argument. For example, the previous statement could be written in many different but semantically equivalent ways:

```
5 = X
X + 1 = 6
3 × X = X + 10
```

Our temperature-conversion program also could be expressed in many equivalent forms. In fact, we might have forgotten the equation for the relationship between F and C, but remember the following information:

- The relationship is linear (it can be expressed as an equation of the form "$y = m \cdot x + b$").

- 212 degrees Fahrenheit is the same temperature as 100 degrees Celsius (the boiling point of water).

- 32 degrees Fahrenheit is the same temperature as 0 degrees Celsius (the freezing point of water).

This information is easily expressed as the following three constraints:

```
F = M×C + B
212 = M×100 + B
32 = M×0 + B
```

The constraint-satisfaction system will determine the appropriate values for M and B using the last two constraints, and plug them into the first constraint, yielding the desired F = 1.8×C + 32. Constraint languages allow the user greater *expressiveness*, because a program can be stated in whichever way is most convenient.

The treatment of equality in constraint languages also is more natural to nonprogrammers. For example, the statement (here expressed in FORTRAN)

```
X = X + 1
```

has always been a source of confusion to beginning programmers until they learn about the imperative notion of incrementing variables. This statement would be a contradiction in a constraint language because no finite value can be found to satisfy it. Furthermore, a constraint-satisfaction system can detect that this statement is false without knowing the value of x. The rules of algebra can be used to subtract x from both sides of the equation, yielding $0 = 1$, which evaluates to false. The equivalent FORTRAN expression

```
X .EQ. X + 1
```

if used in a loop that supplies values for x, will be blindly reevaluated to false over and over for each new value of x. The ability to evaluate an expression containing unknown variables to a constant can be used to advantage by a compiler for a constraint language.

Also note that, in a constraint language, the equal sign expresses an invariant (a *constraint*) between objects that is permanent during the program's execution. In a conventional language, the only time a relation expressed by an assignment statement is guaranteed to hold is just after the statement is executed.

1.1.2 Using Constraints for Computer Graphics

A major advantage of constraint languages is their ability to describe complex objects simply and naturally. As an example, consider the relatively simple task of drawing a regular pentagon using some computer graphics system.

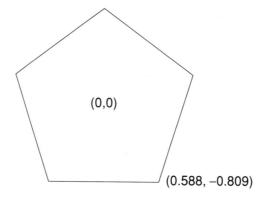

Figure 1.1   Drawing a regular pentagon

This would be very difficult (if not impossible) to do with any degree of accuracy using a typical interactive graphics system such as MacPaint [Kaehler 1983]. With a typical procedural graphics system, such as PIC [Kernighan 1982] or GKS [ISO 1981], this task is reasonable, but the user must specify how to draw the pentagon by specifying the endpoints of the lines. These endpoints must be calculated using trigonometric functions, and they depend on the location, size, and orientation of the pentagon. For example, if an upright pentagon of unit radius is centered at the point (0, 0), then the lower-right corner is approximately at (0.588, –0.809), as in Figure 1.1. We could possibly specify the endpoints relative to the center of the pentagon, or as a function of the size or even the orientation of the pentagon, but this would be quite a bit of work for a user who just wanted to draw a simple figure.

With a constraint language, a regular pentagon could be specified by drawing any five-sided convex polygon, constraining the vertices to lie on a circle as in Figure 1.2 (or equivalently, to be of equal distance from a point), and constraining the edges to be of equal length.

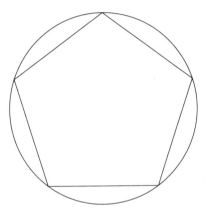

Figure 1.2   Describing a regular pentagon

This not only is easier to do, but also results in a more concise description because it does not depend on any extraneous information, such as the location, size, or orientation of the pentagon. It also does not constrain the order in which the sides of the pentagon are drawn (for example, to allow a program to optimize pen movement for a plotter). Finally, it is much easier to generalize the constraint description to other regular polygons. If desired, constraints can be placed on the location and size of the figure by constraining the location and size of the circle (note that these constraints are independent of the number of sides in the figure). We can also place constraints on the orientation of the figure, for example by constraining the x coordinates of the top point of the figure and the center of the circle to be equal, or by constraining the bottom to be horizontal.

The declarative semantics of constraint languages allow us to describe graphical objects while avoiding extraneous concerns about the algorithms used to draw them. Graphics imagery especially benefits from this because it is inherently spatial and is produced only grudgingly by current procedural languages.

1.2 Scope of the Research

This section defines more precisely some of the terms that have been used informally in the preceeding discussion. A **constraint** expresses a desired relationship among one or more objects. A **constraint language** is the language used to describe the objects and the constraints. A **constraint-language program** is a program written in a constraint language; this program defines a set of objects and set of constraints on these objects. A **constraint-satisfaction system** finds solutions to constraint-language programs. The constraint-satisfaction system uses problem-solving methods, called **constraint-satisfaction techniques**, to find the values of the objects that will make the relationships true.

These definitions are broad and can be interpreted to include a wide variety of systems, from languages that allow some constraintlike statements, to special-purpose systems that satisfy relations between objects. For example, some imperative programming languages (such as Euclid and Common LISP) have an ASSERT statement, and even FORTRAN has an EQUIVALENCE statement that effectively asserts that two variables are always equal. Also included by these definitions would be languages such as the graphics language PIC [Kernighan 1982] and spread-sheet languages which allow relations to be specified, but require that these relations be ordered so that the values of the variables can be calculated in a single pass. At the opposite end of the spectrum allowed by these definitions, symbolic-algebra systems can solve systems of simultaneous equations, and integer programming techniques can be used to find optimal solutions to systems of inequalities.

This book describes an emerging class of (possibly general-purpose) programming languages that use constraint-satisfaction techniques, which I will call **constraint programming languages**. From this designation, I will exclude a vast number of programming languages that use constraint-satisfaction techniques incidentally, or that allow constraints, but require the user to indicate how they are to be solved (typically by ordering them), and will consider only those declarative languages that use constraint satisfaction as their primary computation mechanism. I will also consider only those constraint languages that can reasonably be called programming languages, as opposed to systems that solve constraints but are not generally considered to be programming languages, such as typical symbolic-algebra systems. This distinction may seem arbitrary, but it is analogous to the distinction between logic programming languages such as Prolog, and resolution theorem-proving systems.

I will also concentrate on languages that deal primarily with numeric constraints, and will deal only briefly with languages that use searching techniques to solve logical constraints, such as Prolog. In the future, however, these two classes of languages may not be so distinct. There are already languages being proposed that may be able to deal with both types of constraints. For the present, however, we will concentrate on techniques for solving numeric constraints.

As is true of most programming languages, a major concern will be the execution speed of constraint programming languages. For example, some constraint-satisfaction techniques will be of interest despite their weak problem-solving abilities because they can be interpreted quickly, or are amenable for compilation. The ability to compile constraint programs will be of major interest in evaluating constraint-satisfaction techniques.

This book will consider only numeric constraint programming languages and constraint-satisfaction systems. Therefore, unless otherwise noted, I will use the shorter terms **constraint language** and **constraint-satisfaction system** to refer to such languages and the systems that interpret them. I also will consider only those constraint-satisfaction techniques that are suitable for implementing these constraint languages. Many potential constraint-satisfaction techniques will not be discussed (or will be only mentioned briefly) simply because they are too slow to be used by a programming language.

1.3 Problem Solving versus Constraint Programming

Because of the high level of specification possible in constraint languages, it is much easier to state constraints than to satisfy them. This is in contrast to conventional imperative languages, where it is relatively easy for the compiler to "satisfy" a correctly specified algorithm. In a constraint language, it is easy to specify correctly problems that any constraint satisfier cannot solve. For example, consider the following constraints:

$$x^n + y^n = z^n$$
$$x, y, z, n \text{ are positive integers}$$
$$n > 2$$

Finding a set of values that satisfies these constraints would constitute a counterexample to Fermat's last theorem. This is obviously an extreme example, but there are many problems, easily solvable by human problem solvers, or even by special-purpose computer programs, that cannot be solved by currently used constraint-satisfaction techniques.

The descriptive nature of constraint languages makes it easy to describe problems, which is one of their major advantages, but it also makes it tempting simply to express a problem to a constraint-satisfaction system and then expect it to be solved automatically. Constraint-satisfaction systems, however, are *not* meant to be general-purpose problem solvers. They are not even as powerful as many mechanical problem solvers, such as symbolic-algebra systems. Constraint-satisfaction systems are meant to solve quickly and efficiently the little, trivial problems that surround and obscure more difficult problems. This frees the user's problem-solving skills for use on the more interesting problems. Thus constraint-satisfaction systems should not be thought of as problem solvers; they are tools to help humans solve problems.

This is not to say that constraint languages cannot be used to solve difficult problems. After all, languages such as LISP have no problem-solving abilities at all, but they can be used to build powerful symbolic-algebra systems and other problem solvers. Constraint languages add a small amount of problem-solving skill, and so reduce the size and difficulty of the task the user must deal with. This is roughly analogous to the way that LISP systems automatically take care of garbage collection, so the user need not be concerned with the management of storage. With LISP, we pay for automatic storage management by giving up some execution speed. With constraint languages, because most problem-solving methods are application specific, we give up some programming generality.

An Example

What a constraint language can do is to make it easier for a human problem solver to describe a problem to a computer, and thus make it easier to apply the computer's abilities to the problem. For example, calculating the voltages at the nodes of a small network of resistors requires the solution of a few dozen simultaneous equations. There are several possible approaches (ignoring constraint languages) to finding the solution for such a problem:

- Set up the equations and solve them by hand. This is what most people would do, but it is a tedious and error-prone task.

- Write a program in an imperative language to calculate the voltages. Unfortunately, writing an imperative program to solve simultaneous equations is more difficult, and just as error-prone, as solving the equations by hand. Writing such a program would be worthwhile only if the user needed to solve many problems of this type.

- Use an existing special-purpose problem solver, such as a symbolic-algebra system, to solve the simultaneous equations. The user would still have to figure out what the simultaneous equations are from the circuit, and each change to the circuit will require a new set of equations.

Using a constraint language, this problem can be described simply as a network of connected resistors, and the constraint-satisfaction system can set up the simultaneous equations automatically (an example of this is given in Section 5.7). This allows the user to concentrate on designing the circuit. While it is performing the calculations for the voltages, the constraint satisfier can also check to make sure that we do not burn up a resistor by putting too much power through it. A human problem solver should not be bothered with such details.

In general, the issue is not *how difficult* are the problems that a constraint-satisfaction system can solve, but rather *how efficiently* can the constraints of interest be solved. What the constraints of interest are depends on the application. Another issue is how easy is it for the constraints of interest to be stated to the constraint-satisfaction system. If a constraint language is general-purpose and extensible, then the user can tailor the language to the application, making the constraints of interest to the specific application easier to state.

1.4 Limitations of Existing Constraint Languages

Problem-solving systems are typically very difficult to implement, and constraint-satisfaction systems are no exception. Even though constraint languages have been around for over twenty years, relatively few systems to execute them have been built in that time. Graphics researchers are still praising Ivan Sutherland's Sketchpad system [Sutherland 1963], built in the early 1960s, but few have attempted to duplicate it. Furthermore, the constraint-satisfaction systems that have been built tend to be very application specific and hard to adapt to other, or more general, tasks. Consequently, despite the significant contributions of existing constraint languages, they have not found wide acceptance or use. There are several causes of this problem, and existing constraint languages suffer from one or more of them:

- General problem-solving techniques are weak, so constraint-satisfaction systems must use application-dependent techniques. It is usually difficult to change or modify these systems to suit other applications. The few constraint languages that can be adapted to new applications are adaptable only by dropping down into their implementation language. For example, the ThingLab simulation laboratory [Borning 1981] allows an experienced programmer to build simulations (which in effect are small constraint-satisfaction systems for solving limited classes of problems) by defining new objects and constraints, but these new constraints must be defined procedurally, using Smalltalk.*

- The data types operated on by typical constraint languages are fixed. There is no way to build up new data types (such as by using *records* or *arrays* as in conventional languages). For example, in Juno [Nelson 1985], an interactive graphics constraint language, the only data type is a two-dimensional point. In order to use Juno for even a slightly different application, such as three-dimensional graphics, the underlying system would have to be modified extensively.

---

* Recent enhancements allow some constraints to be defined functionally or graphically [Borning 1985a, 1985b].

- Some constraint languages allow the definition of new data types, but new constraints that utilize these new data types cannot be added. New constraints correspond to procedures in conventional languages. In IDEAL [Van Wyk 1982], another graphics constraint language, the only primitive data type is a point, but new data types such as lines, arrows, and rectangles can be defined. Relations between the nonprimitive data types, however, must be expressed in terms of primitives (points). So, for example, to draw an arrow between two rectangles, separate constraints must be expressed connecting the head and tail of the arrow to the desired points on the rectangles. This is only a limitation on expressiveness, but, like a conventional language without subroutines, it does tend to make a constraint language unwieldy. It also takes away some of the benefit of using a constraint language. For example, it is of little advantage when a constraint language allows us to define a new data type for a resistor if we then have to describe each connection between resistors in terms of primitive constraints between their voltages and currents. We would much rather be able to define constraints for connecting resistors together.

- Many existing constraint languages do not allow any computations to be expressed beyond what can be expressed by a conjunction of primitive constraints. So even if new constraints can be added to the language, these new constraints may be severely limited. In Juno, for example, new constraints can be added as long as they can be expressed as a conjunction of Juno's four primitive constraints. One of Juno's primitives asserts that two line segments are to be of equal length, so we can add a constraint that two line segments are perpendicular by using the standard geometric construction of a perpendicular bisector. Unfortunately, there is no way to express *betweenness* (for example, that a point lies between two other points on a line). This constraint could be expressed if we could only say that the *sum* of two distances is equal to a third distance, but we cannot compute sums. Consequently, many objects cannot be uniquely specified. For example, given the constraints that we used to define a pentagon in Section 1.1.2, Juno might instead produce a pentagram (five-sided star), since Juno does not allow constraints on the relative order of the vertices.

- Even in constraint languages that do allow computation (such as IDEAL, which includes the normal complement of arithmetic operators), few are computationally complete. This is a consequence of the difficulty of adding control structures (such as conditionals, iteration, or recursion) to a nonprocedural language, such as a constraint language, without adding any procedural semantics. Consequently, there are computable functions that these languages cannot compute. For example, without iteration (or recursion) it is impossible to express the general concept of a dashed line (where the number of line segments is not fixed). To solve this problem, IDEAL had to add a new primitive (the *pen* statement) that is a much restricted form of an iterator. The few constraint languages that are computationally complete are so only because they allow the constraint programmer to drop down into an imperative language (typically LISP or Smalltalk). Unfortunately, this also destroys the declarative semantics of the constraint language. It is possible to add control structures to a declarative language without adding procedural semantics (as in Lucid [Wadge 1985], Pure LISP, and others), so it should be possible to add them to a constraint language.

- Even if we do not require computational completeness, if our language does not have conditionals then constraints that depend on other constraints cannot be expressed. Such constraints (called **higher-order constraints**, discussed in Section 2.2) allow us to tailor the solution of a set of constraints to different circumstances. For example, we might wish to express a constraint that centers some text inside a rectangle, unless the width of the text is too wide, in which case the text is to be broken onto multiple lines.

- Many constraint-satisfaction systems use iterative numeric techniques such as relaxation. These techniques can have numerical-stability problems; a system using these techniques might fail to terminate even when the constraints have a solution, or might find one solution arbitrarily for constraints with more than one solution. For example, Juno uses Newton–Raphson iteration for satisfying constraints and so for the pentagon example in Section 1.1.2 it will arbitrarily return either the desired regular pentagon or a pentagram depending on the shape of the initial polygon. This can lead to unexpected changes to the result when some only slightly related constraint is modified. Also, this means that the answer might depend on the order in which the constraints are solved, which effectively destroys any declarative semantics.

In summary, systems to execute constraint languages are difficult to implement, and once one is implemented we are typically stuck with a special-purpose language that, suffering from one or more of the above problems, is just as difficult to modify to apply to other applications. What is needed is an easier way to implement constraint languages, which also avoids all of the above problems. We would like the languages so implemented to be computationally complete (while retaining purely declarative semantics, of course), so we can handle any constraint whose solution is computable, including higher-order constraints. In addition, something like abstract data types would allow new data types and constraints to be defined. And, of course, it must be fast.

One possible approach would be to generate constraint-satisfaction systems using a rule-based specification language — similar to the way parsers can be built by parser generators that accept specifications in the form of grammar rules. Of course, in order to specify a constraint-satisfaction system, not only must we specify the syntax of the constraint language (as for a parser), we must also specify its semantics (what the constraints mean), and, even more difficult, we must give rules that specify how to satisfy the constraints. In order to have abstract data types, we must also be able to define new data types, and be able to control the application of rules to objects based on their type.

1.5 Proposed Solution

This book presents a general-purpose language called **Bertrand** (after Bertrand Russell), which is a solution to the problem of building constraint-satisfaction systems. Bertrand is a rule-based specification language — a constraint satisfaction system is specified as a set of rules and is automatically generated from those rules. Bertrand allows new constraints to be defined, and also has a form of abstract data type.

The major goal of this book is to show that Bertrand makes it easier to build constraint-satisfaction systems. In order to demonstrate how easy it is to build constraint-satisfaction systems using this language, we will examine how existing constraint languages would be used to solve some example problems,* and then generate a constraint language using Bertrand to solve the same problems. These examples will also serve to show that the constraint languages generated using Bertrand are as powerful as existing constraint languages.

The mechanism used to interpret the rules specifying a constraint-satisfaction system is a form of term rewriting. Term rewriting [Bundy 1983] has been used to build interpreters for languages other than constraint languages. For example, the equational interpreter, a term rewriting system developed by Hoffmann and O'Donnell at Purdue, has been used to build interpreters for LISP and Lucid [Hoffmann 1982]. Bertrand uses an extended form of term rewriting, which I call **augmented term rewriting**. Within the framework of term rewriting, augmented term rewriting includes the ability to bind values to variables, and to define abstract data types. These extensions make term rewriting powerful enough that it can be used to build interpreters for constraint languages.

Augmented term rewriting shares with standard term rewriting several desirable properties: it is general-purpose and has a simple operational semantics, which makes it easy to execute. In addition, augmented term rewriting has properties that make it possible to take advantage of well-known optimizations, so the same mechanism also helps solve the execution-speed problem. It can be implemented efficiently as an interpreter using fast pattern-matching techniques, or compiled to run on a conventional processor or even a parallel processor such as a data-flow computer.

---

* In most cases, the problems will be substantial examples taken from the thesis or other document describing the existing constraint language.

Constraint-satisfaction systems can be easily described using Bertrand and efficiently implemented using augmented term rewriting.

The remainder of this book is divided as follows:

- Chapter 2 discusses existing constraint-satisfaction techniques. These techniques will be used to build constraint-satisfaction systems using Bertrand.

- Chapter 3 describes augmented term rewriting, especially how it differs from standard term rewriting. This chapter also introduces the Bertrand programming language, shows its connection to augmented term rewriting, and gives some examples of its use.

- Chapter 4 describes existing constraint languages, and presents example problems for them to solve. In Chapters 5 and 6, constraint languages will be built using Bertrand to solve these same problems.

- Chapter 5 uses Bertrand to build an equation solver based on algebraic transformation techniques. This algebraic constraint-satisfaction system is used as a base on which the other constraint languages are built to solve the example problems.

- Chapter 6 discusses how graphic input and output can be added to Bertrand, and uses the resulting language to solve constraint problems involving graphics.

- Chapter 7 discusses how augmented term rewriting is amenable for efficient execution, including showing how parallelism can be detected and utilized.

- Appendix A gives further examples of constraint languages built using Bertrand, including listings of the rules for a simultaneous equation solver and a graphics library.

- Appendix B presents a formal operational semantics for augmented term rewriting, and discusses its properties.

- Appendix C gives the code for a working interpreter for an augmented term rewriting system.

Chapter 2

Constraint Satisfaction

2.1 Constraint-Satisfaction Techniques

Constraint satisfaction, like most techniques for solving problems, is composed of two distinct parts: a set of problem-solving rules, and a control mechanism.* The problem-solving rules can be fairly general-purpose, such as the rules of arithmetic and algebra, or they can be more application-specific. The control mechanism controls when and how the rules are applied.

Unfortunately, most constraint-satisfaction systems do not strongly distinguish between the control mechanism and the problem-solving rules. This has been a major contributer to the difficulty of building (and modifying) constraint-satisfaction systems. This situation is similar to the one that once existed for knowledge-based systems, such as MYCIN, which tended to be complex and unwieldy. Later systems, such as EMYCIN [Buchanan 1984], explicitly separated the rules from the control mechanism. Prolog is another example of the benefits of separating the control mechanism (resolution) from the rules (a Prolog program).

The constraints that a constraint-satisfaction system can solve will depend on the problem-solving rules that it can use. If a problem is solvable (i.e., ignoring Fermat's last theorem and other similar problems), then we can come up with a set of rules to solve it. Unfortunately, the kinds of rules that a constraint-satisfaction system can use, and consequently the kinds of problems it can solve, will depend on what control mechanism or mechanisms are used.

We will notice that as constraint-satisfaction techniques get more powerful, they tend to get more domain-specific. This trade-off is due to the weakness of general problem-solving methods. The problems we can solve will depend on the sophistication of our tools. By analogy, we can fix quite a few things with a pair of pliers and a screwdriver, but there are times when more sophisticated application-specific tools are necessary.

---

* Kowalski says that "Algorithm = Logic + Control", in that in a logic programming language an algorithm consists of both a logic (descriptive) part and a control (procedural) part [Kowalski 1979]. Since constraint languages are declarative, the control part is either hidden from the user, or specified declaratively. Thus in a constraint language "Algorithm = Logic", but the logic may also (logically) specify some control information.

The rest of this chapter will examine the control mechanisms that have been used by existing constraint-satisfaction systems, and discuss the types of problems that can be handled by each mechanism.

2.1.1 Constraint Graphs

A constraint-language program can be regarded as a graph. For example, Figure 2.1 is a graphical representation of the program $C \times 1.8 + 32 = F$.

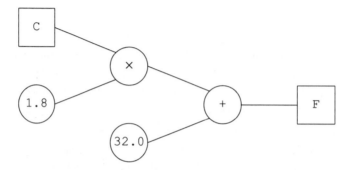

Figure 2.1   Graphical representation of the temperature-conversion program

The square nodes represent objects (variables), and the round nodes represent operators. The arguments to an operator are attached on its left side, and the result is attached on its right side. Operators that take no arguments (nullary operators) are constants.

Note that the "equal to" operator (=) is not represented explicitly in the constraint graph. It is required in the textual form of expressions because our infix functional notation for operators has no explicit representation for the result of an operator. If we represented operators as relations (for example, $a+b=c$ as `plus (a,b,c)`) then the equal sign would not be required, but we would have to give names to all the arcs in a program. The resulting programs would also be much more difficult to read.

2.1.2 Local Propagation

The simplest and easiest-to-implement constraint-satisfaction mechanism is called **local propagation of known states**, or just local propagation [Steele 1979]. In this mechanism, known values are propagated along the arcs. When a node receives sufficient information from its arcs, it *fires*, calculates one or more values for the arcs that do not contain values, and sends these new values out. These new values then propagate along the arcs, causing new nodes to fire, and so on.

The problem-solving rules are local to each node, and only involve information contained on the arcs connected to that node. A constant node contains all the information it needs, so it can fire immediately and send its value out. A "plus" node can fire when two of its arcs contain values. For example, if a plus node is connected to arcs named p, q, and r, so that the constraint is p+q=r, then the node will contain the rules:

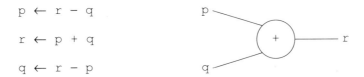

$$p \leftarrow r - q$$
$$r \leftarrow p + q$$
$$q \leftarrow r - p$$

Figure 2.2   The rules for a plus node

Which rule to apply will depend on which arcs receive values. For example, if values arrive on arcs q and r, then the rule $p \leftarrow r - q$ will be triggered.

Choosing which rule to fire for a "plus" node is dependent only on which arcs receive values, but rule firing can depend on other information. For example, under certain conditions a "times" node can fire when only one of its arcs receives a value. If a value arrives on either p or q, and that value is equal to zero, then a zero can be sent out over r without waiting for a value on the other arc.

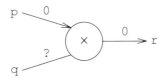

Figure 2.3   Propagating zero through a times node

The arrows in Figure 2.3 indicate the direction values travel on the arcs. If values arrived on both arcs p and q, and one of those values was equal to zero, then either of two rules could be used. In this case both rules would have the same effect, but this is not always true. If more than one rule could be applied in a given situation there must be some way to choose one over another. A typical way to do this is to pick the rule that is first in textual order.*

---

* Note that this is not the same as specifying the order in which constraints are to be solved (for example, by specifying the order in which the nodes are to fire), and does not necessarily harm the declarative semantics of a constraint language.

Temperature Conversion Solved Using Local Propagation

In the temperature-conversion program, initially both constant nodes fire and send their values out. Since the constant 1.8 is not zero, the times node cannot fire, and the system waits until either F or C is assigned a value. If C is assigned the value 10, this value is propagated to the times node, which fires and sends the value 18 to the plus node, which also fires and sends the value 50 to the F node, and the system is solved.

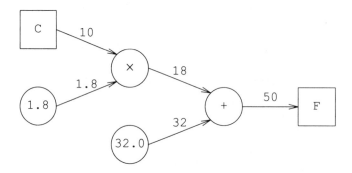

Figure 2.4   The Fahrenheit value of 10 degrees Celsius

If instead, F were assigned the value −40, then this value is propagated to the plus node, which fires and sends the value −72 to the times node, which also fires and sends the value −40 to the C node, and the system is solved.

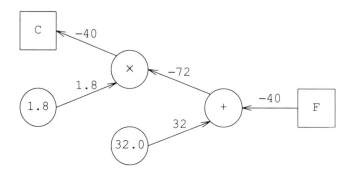

Figure 2.5   The Celsius value of −40 degrees Fahrenheit

Note that operators in a constraint program will often be used backwards to compute what an argument must be for a given result. This, of course, is not always possible. For example, for a times node, if the result and one of the arguments are both zero then no information can be deduced about the other argument. This is not a fault with local propagation; no constraint-satisfaction mechanism could deduce anything in this situation. Table 2.1 shows a complete list of rules for a times node.

Table 2.1	
trigger	rule
p, p = 0	r ← 0
q, q = 0	r ← 0
q, r, q ≠ 0	p ← r / q
p, r, p ≠ 0	q ← r / p
p, q	r ← p × q

Explanations

One advantage of local-propagation techniques is that the system can keep track of which rule in a node caused the node to fire. This information can be used to give *explanations* for why the system gave a particular answer. For example, we could ask the system why, in the example above, it said that the value of C was −40, and it could answer with something like

```
because −40 is −72 / 1.8,
1.8 is a constant,
−72 is −40 − 32,
32 is a constant,
and −40 was given as the value of F.
```

Constraint Graphs Containing Cycles

The major disadvantage of local-propagation techniques is that they can only use information local to a node. Many common constraint problems cannot be solved this way. For example, consider a constraint program for finding the average of two numbers:

$$A + T = B$$
$$B + T = C$$

This program constrains B to be the average of A and C, and T to be the difference between A and B (which is also the difference between B and C). As shown in Figure 2.6, the constraint graph for this program contains a cycle.

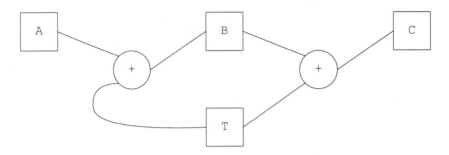

Figure 2.6   Constraint graph containing a cycle

If values are given to the two variables A and C, local propagation is unable to solve for the values of either B or T. For example, if A is 1 and C is 11, then the equations become

$$1 \ + \ T \ = \ B$$
$$B \ + \ T \ = \ 11$$

Neither equation, individually, can be solved because there is a cyclic dependency between B and T, and more global information is required to deduce values for either variable. Looking at Figure 2.7, we can see that B and T are in a cycle. If we do not give a value to either B or T, then neither plus node can fire, so local propagation cannot break the cycle.

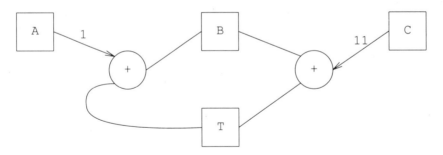

Figure 2.7   Local propagation cannot solve graphs containing cycles

At this point, local propagation will give up, and say that the program has no solution. Of course, there is a solution, but more-powerful techniques must be used to find it.

2.1.3 Relaxation

One method that can solve the above program is a classical iterative numerical-approximation technique called **relaxation** [Sutherland 1963]. Relaxation makes an initial guess at the values of the unknown objects, and then estimates the error that would be caused by assigning these values to the objects. New guesses are then made, and new error estimates calculated, and this process repeats until the error is minimized. Different forms of relaxation will use different heuristics to make the guesses. One way to make the new guesses is to perturb the value of each object in turn, and watch what happens to the error estimate.

A form of relaxation used in several constraint-satisfaction systems assumes that the errors for each constrained object can be reasonably approximated by some linear function. To determine the new guess for the value of each object, the derivative of each error function is approximated with a linear function. Then a least squares fit is performed on the linear functions for each object. This process is repeated in turn for each variable until the error terms converge to zero. If the error terms do not converge, then relaxation fails. An advantage of iterative techniques such as relaxation is that even if the error terms do not go to zero they can often be minimized, so these techniques can be used to find approximate solutions to overconstrained problems.

Relaxation can only be used on objects with continuous numeric values, and not on Boolean or even integer-valued objects. For example, it cannot solve cryptarithmetic problems. (Cryptarithmetic involves finding an assignment of numeric digits to letters to satisfy some constraint, for example "SEND + MORE = MONEY".) Even so, the class of problems it can solve is quite large. A further limitation is that the constraints to be relaxed must be able to be approximated adequately by linear equations, otherwise relaxation may not converge, or there may be more than one solution and relaxation will arbitrarily find one of them. Even for systems of linear equations, which are guaranteed to converge, relaxation is usually very slow. For nonlinear systems of equations, whether or not relaxation converges and the rate of convergence are very sensitive to a number of factors, including the number of variables to be relaxed, the choice of initial values and the form of the constraint graph. Relaxation can be used directly as a constraint-satisfaction mechanism, but because it is slow, relaxation is often used only after local propagation has been tried and failed.

Average of Two Numbers Problem Solved Using Relaxation

There are a number of tricks that can be used to speed up relaxation when used in combination with local-propagation techniques. One of these techniques reduces the number of objects that need to be relaxed by picking one of them, and then determining what other values could be deduced using local propagation if the value of that one were known. The values that can be deduced do not need to be guessed at for each iteration of relaxation, although their error terms need to be considered. This technique can be used on our constraint program that finds the average of 1 and 11.

If naive relaxation were used, then both B and T would have to be relaxed. Instead, let us pick B to be relaxed, and for an initial guess set its value to zero. As shown in Figure 2.8, if the zero propagates to the second plus node, that node fires and sets the value of T to 11. This value then propagates to the first plus node, which fires and sends out 12 as the value of B.

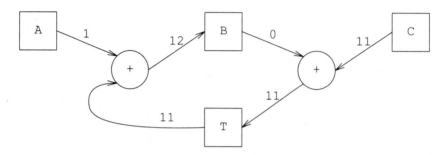

Figure 2.8   Relaxation

Now B has two values, the initial guess (zero), and the value that was propagated back (12). The error for B is the difference between these two values, and the new guess for the value of B is just the average of the two.* The average of 12 and 0 is 6, which is the right value. To check that it is the right value, we propagate it around the loop again to see that it comes back unchanged. This final propagation step also determines the value of T to be 5.

In general, this method will converge in one iteration if the constraints are linear. In this example, I picked a particular order for the propagation, but any order would have worked. Note that if the initial guess of 0 for B had been propagated to both plus nodes, then T would have received two values, –1 and 11, so it is important to consider the error term for T as well as for B.

2.1.4 Propagating Degrees of Freedom

Another problem with naive relaxation is that much more of a graph might be relaxed than is necessary. Since relaxation has no global information about the graph there is no way for it to tell which variables are in a cycle and which are just in branches connected to the cycle. For a large graph, this can result in a significant overhead. For example, consider the following constraint program:

$$5 \times Y = X$$
$$X + X = 40$$

---

* In order to solve a constraint program to find the average of two numbers, relaxation ends up taking the average of two (different) numbers.

This program corresponds to the following graph:

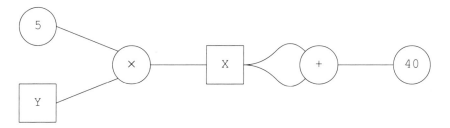

Figure 2.9   A graph containing a small cycle

In the graph in Figure 2.9, nothing can be deduced using local propagation because the constraint X + X = 40 contains a cycle. Relaxation can be used to find the value of X, but other variables, such as Y, that are in branches connected to the cycle will be relaxed as well. Here the branch containing Y is fairly small and will only cause a single extra variable to be relaxed, but if the branch was very large, possibly containing hundreds of variables, all of them would be subject to relaxation, resulting in extremely poor performance.

One way to avoid this problem is to prune the branches connected to cycles temporarily during an initial local-propagation step. Then relaxation is only done on the variables inside cycles. After relaxation has determined the value of variables inside cycles, these values are propagated back out to the branches. In order to do the pruning, **local propagation of degrees of freedom** is used. Instead of looking for an object whose value is known and propagating its value, this technique looks for an object with few enough constraints so that its value can be changed to satisfy its constraints. When a part with enough degrees of freedom is found it is removed from the constraint graph, along with all the constraints that apply to it.

For example, in the above graph, the object X has three constraints on it, but the object Y has only a single constraint, so once the value of X is known, it is possible to satisfy the constraint 5 × Y = X by changing the value of Y. The object Y can therefore be removed from the constraint graph, along with the times node and the constant 5. What remains is just the cycle containing the object X. Relaxation can be used on this cycle to determine that X is equal to 20, then the pruned branch is restored and local propagation of known states is used to determine that the value of Y is 4.

One difficulty with this technique is determining which objects have enough degrees of freedom. Typically, the heuristic used is that a variable has enough degrees of freedom if it has only one constraint on it. Note that it is not important whether the constraint will uniquely determine the value of the object during the final propagation-of-values step.

Precompilation

A further refinement of this technique is to precompile the final propagation step. This compilation is done while propagating degrees of freedom. When an object is pruned from the graph, a **one-step deduction** is compiled that is a procedure for determining the value of the object. For example, when the branch containing Y is pruned, the deduction $Y \leftarrow X/5$ is compiled by taking the appropriate rule from the times node and replacing the arc names with the appropriate objects. After relaxation is finished, this rule can be used directly to compute the value of Y, completely avoiding the final local-propagation step.

Propagating degrees of freedom has an advantage over propagating known states even if the graph does not contain any cycles. Consider again the graph of the temperature-conversion program, in Figure 2.10.

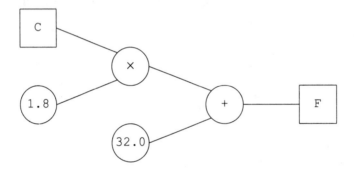

Figure 2.10   Initial graph of the temperature-conversion program

If we want to use this program to find the Celsius equivalent of several Fahrenheit temperatures, it can be precompiled by propagating degrees of freedom. Since F is our input, only the object C has enough degrees of freedom. We remove C and its associated constraint, and compile the deduction $C \leftarrow T1/1.8$, where T1 is a temporary variable. The graph now looks like Figure 2.11.

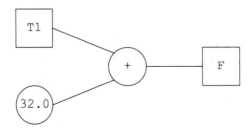

Figure 2.11   After the first deduction has been compiled

We continue removing constraints until the graph is empty. The variable T1 has enough degrees of freedom, so we can remove it and its associated constraint, and compile the deduction T1 ← F − 32. The graph is now empty, and we have compiled the deductions T1 ← F − 32 and C ← T1/1.8, which together form the procedure C ← (F − 32)/1.8. This procedure can be used to calculate the Celsius equivalent of several different Fahrenheit temperatures. If we had used local propagation of known states, then a complete propagation would be required for each new value of F.

Limitations of Propagation of Degrees of Freedom

Propagating degrees of freedom is slightly less powerful than propagating known states because we cannot take advantage of rules that use information about the values on arcs, such as the rule in the times node for multiplying by zero. Consequently, propagating degrees of freedom must use relaxation on all cycles, even if the cycle could have been broken (or even ignored completely), for example, by a fortuitous multiplication by zero.

2.1.5 Redundant Views

Relaxation can often be avoided if the user supplies a redundant view of a constraint that can be solved using local propagation. For example, consider the constraint program from above that had to be solved using relaxation:

$$5 \times Y = X$$
$$X + X = 40$$

The constraint X + X = 40 cannot be solved using local propagation because it contains a cycle. It could have been solved, however, if the user supplied the equivalent constraint:

$$2 \times X = 40$$

The constraint program for finding the average of two numbers:

$$A + T = B$$
$$B + T = C$$

could also have been solved without relaxation by supplying either (or even both) of the following redundant constraints:

$$B = (A + C) / 2$$
$$A + T \times 2 = C$$

Adding the latter constraint to the original program creates the graph in Figure 2.12.

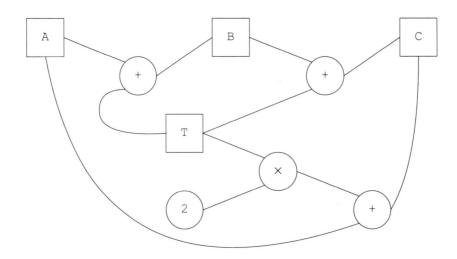

Figure 2.12   Redundant view added to a graph

This graph can be solved using local propagation if any two of the variables (A, B, C, and T) are supplied.

Redundant views can also be used to help solve constraint problems that cannot be solved using relaxation. In some sense, redundant views allow the user to help the constraint-satisfaction system solve problems that are too difficult for it to solve by itself. This is one way in which a user can tailor a constraint-satisfaction system to a particular application.

Of course, rather than have the user supply the redundant views, we would rather have them generated automatically for us. A system could use some local-propagation technique to find parts of a graph that it cannot solve, and then try to transform those subgraphs into graphs that can be solved.

2.1.6 Graph Transformation

Graph transformation (also called term rewriting) uses rewrite rules to transform subgraphs of a constraint program into other (hopefully simpler) graphs. For example, the rewrite rule

$$V + V \Rightarrow 2 \times V$$

where V is a variable that can match any expression, can be used to transform the expression X + X (from the example in the last section), into $2 \times X$. Other rules can be used to implement such things as the distributive law.

Temperature Conversion Solved Using Graph Transformation

In addition to using graph transformation to transform difficult parts of constraint graphs, it can be used to replace local propagation entirely. This is done by replacing operators whose arcs contain constants with the equivalent constant. For example, in the temperature-conversion program in Figure 2.13, if F is given the value 32

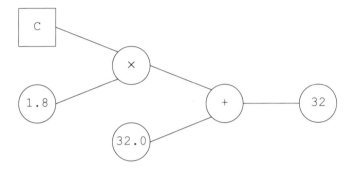

Figure 2.13   F replaced by the constant 32

the plus operator can be transformed away, leaving the graph in Figure 2.14.

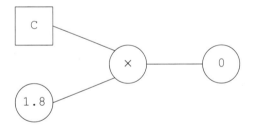

Figure 2.14   After the first transformation

This graph can then be transformed to a single constant zero — the answer to the problem.

Transforming Cycles

Graph transformation is more powerful than local propagation because it can look at more of the constraint graph. Local propagation is limited to looking at only a single node and the values on its arcs. Unfortunately, transformation is still limited to looking at locally connected subgraphs, so it can only transform simple cycles in a constraint graph (such as $X + X$). Cycles formed by simultaneous equations, except for a few trivial cases, cannot be solved using graph-transformation techniques because these cycles are typically not local in extent. In order to get around this limitation we need more-sophisticated equation-solving techniques.

2.1.7 Equation Solving

The equation-solving techniques used in symbolic-algebra systems (such as
MACSYMA [MathLab 1983]) can be used to solve complex constraint programs
(including programs containing cycles), but are too slow to be considered as a
general-purpose constraint-satisfaction mechanism. Consequently, equation-solving
techniques are often used like relaxation techniques — only after local propagation
has failed. If an equation-solving technique existed that would execute fast enough,
however, we could consider dispensing with local propagation entirely.

To develop such a technique, let us examine how simultaneous equations are
typically solved by human problem solvers. The most commonly used method of solving simultaneous linear equations is Gaussian elimination. For example, consider
how the following two equations might be solved:

$$p + 2 \times p + 5 \times q = 14$$
$$p - q = 2$$

The subexpression $p + 2 \times p$ contains a cycle that can be removed by combining
terms. We now have two simultaneous equations in two unknowns:

$$3 \times p + 5 \times q = 14$$
$$p - q = 2$$

We can now solve one of the equations for one of the unknowns in terms of the other.
For example, we can solve the second equation for p in terms of q, yielding $2 + q$. We
next replace p in the first equation by its value, leaving us with one equation in one
unknown, which we can solve directly for the value of q. Once we know q, we can
plug it back into our solution for p, yielding values for both p and q in terms of constants.

A Simple Equation Solver

Gaussian elimination can be used as the basis for a simple equation solving algorithm. The algorithm works by attempting to convert each equation into an **ordered
linear combination** [Derman 1984]. An ordered linear combination is a linear
expression whose variables have been ordered. The ordering may be lexicographic by
variable name, or may use any other method that gives a total ordering between distinct variables. From here on I will assume lexicographic ordering, with the constant
term preceding all others. For example, the expression

$$2 \times q + 3 \times r + 4 + 5 \times p$$

is equivalent to the ordered linear combination

$$4 + 5 \times p + 2 \times q + 3 \times r$$

An ordered linear combination can be multiplied by a constant in linear time by multiplying every term in the ordered linear combination by the constant. Likewise, an ordered linear combination can be divided by a constant. Since the variables in an ordered linear combination are kept in sorted order, two ordered linear combinations can be added together in linear time by simply merging them. If the same variable appears in a term in both ordered linear combinations, then their respective constants are added together in the merged result. The difference of two ordered linear combinations can be formed by multiplying the second one by –1, and adding.

Converting an equation into a single ordered linear combination also guarantees that all terms of the same variable have been merged. An equation is converted into an ordered linear combination by traversing, in postorder, the expression tree representing the equation. The leaves of this tree are all either constants or variables — constants already represent (trivial) linear combinations, and each variable x is converted into a linear expression $1 \times x + 0$. As the tree is traversed from the leaves to the root, linear expressions are added together, or multiplied by constants. If the expression tree contains any nonlinear operators, or a multiplication of two nonconstant linear combinations, these are left unconverted in tree form.

Once an equation has been converted into an ordered linear combination that is equal to zero it can be solved (in linear time). There are four possible solutions:

- If the ordered linear combination is the constant zero, it asserts $0 = 0$. This signifies that the original equation was redundant, and we simply throw it away.

- If the ordered linear combination is a constant k not equal to zero, it asserts $k = 0$. For example, if k is 5, then we are asserting $5 = 0$, which is a contradiction. The usual way to handle a contradiction is to signal an error and terminate.

- If the ordered linear combination contains a single variable, say $c \times p + k$, where c and k are constants and p is a variable, then it corresponds to the assertion $p = -k/c$. We set the value of p to be $-k/c$, delete this ordered linear combination, and replace occurrences of p in the other equations by its value $(-k/c)$.

- If the ordered linear combination contains more than one variable, then we pick one of the variables and solve for its value in terms of the other variables. For example, if we are solving the ordered linear combination $\wp$, and the variable p with coefficient c is picked, then we solve for the value of p, which is $(\wp - c \times p)/-c$. Again, wherever the variable p appears in any other equation we replace it by its value. It does not matter which variable is picked to solve for.

If we are using floating-point arithmetic, however, we might want to pick the variable whose coefficient is the largest in absolute value in order to minimize numerical-accuracy problems. This is commonly called *pivoting*.

Temperature Conversion Solved Using Equation Solving

Our temperature-conversion program:

$$\texttt{C} \times \texttt{1.8} \; + \; \texttt{32} \; = \; \texttt{F}$$

is converted into the ordered linear combination:

$$\texttt{32} \; + \; \texttt{1.8} \times \texttt{C} \; + \; \texttt{-1} \times \texttt{F} \; = \; \texttt{0}$$

In order to solve this program, we must somehow supply a value for either F or C. Let us add the additional constraint equation C = 10, resulting in the following two ordered linear combinations:

$$\texttt{32} \; + \; \texttt{1.8} \times \texttt{C} \; + \; \texttt{-1} \times \texttt{F} \; = \; \texttt{0}$$
$$\texttt{-10} \; + \; \texttt{C} \; = \; \texttt{0}$$

We solve these two equations in order. Using pivoting, we solve the first equation for C (the variable with the largest coefficient) and substitute its value into the second, yielding:

$$\texttt{-27.78} \; + \; \texttt{-0.556} \times \texttt{F} \; = \; \texttt{0}$$

which can be solved for the value of F, namely 50.

Instead of giving a constant value to either F or C, let us give the constraint F = C, to find the temperature where the Fahrenheit value is equal to the Celsius value. This results in the following two ordered linear combinations:

$$\texttt{F} \; + \; \texttt{-1} \times \texttt{C} \; = \; \texttt{0}$$
$$\texttt{32} \; + \; \texttt{1.8} \times \texttt{C} \; + \; \texttt{-1} \times \texttt{F} \; = \; \texttt{0}$$

If we solve the first equation for F, we find that its value is just C, which we plug into the second equation to get:

$$\texttt{32} \; + \; \texttt{0.8} \times \texttt{C} \; = \; \texttt{0}$$

This equation can then be solved to find that the value of C is −40 (which is also the value of F, since C = F).

Solving Nonlinear Simultaneous Equations

If the equations to be solved are all linear (the equation trees can all be converted into ordered linear combinations), then this algorithm can solve them in a single pass. The algorithm can also be extended to handle some classes of nonlinear equations. Any equation that cannot be completely converted from an equation tree into an ordered linear combination is placed on a queue, and the remaining equations processed. As linear combinations are solved, a value might become known that will transform a nonlinear equation into a linear one (and allow it to be solved). For example, the three nonlinear simultaneous equations:

$$p \times q = 10$$
$$q + r = 3$$
$$q - r = 1$$

can be solved this way, since when q becomes a constant (by solving the last two equations), the first equation becomes linear. The algorithm continues examining the equations on the queue until they are all solved, or until a pass has been made through them without solving any of them. We call sets of equations that can be solved in this way **slightly-nonlinear simultaneous equations**.

A further extension is to build in some simple nonlinear transformations, such as cross-multiplication and squaring both sides. These can be done using graph transformations. Unfortunately, nonlinear transformations are not always safe to perform. For example, cross-multiplication can return $p = 0$ as the solution of $p = 0/p$, and squaring both sides can cause a negative root to be added. Linear transformations are always safe, but if any nonlinear transformations are used we must be careful to check our answers to make sure they are valid, and do not cause any denominators to vanish.

Limitations of the Simple Equation Solver

A problem with equation solving, which it shares with other graph-transformation techniques, is that it is destructive to the constraint graph. Unlike local propagation, once a graph has been transformed the old graph is lost, unless the old graph is explicitly saved somewhere. Graph transformation makes it difficult to use the same graph repeatedly for different values, or keep track of which rules fired so the system can explain why a certain answer was returned.

This algorithm is not as powerful as the techniques used in symbolic-algebra systems, but it is much faster and easier to implement. In fact, it is almost as easy to implement as local propagation, making it an ideal candidate for a constraint-satisfaction mechanism.

2.1.8 Other Constraint-Satisfaction Techniques

Up until now, this chapter has only discussed constraint-satisfaction techniques that have been used in existing constraint-satisfaction systems, but there are other techniques that could be used. Some of these are related to equation-solving techniques, such as linear programming. Others are based on theorem-proving methods such as resolution. Still others come from artificial intelligence. Searching techniques, such as used in the General Problem Solver [Newell 1963], can be used to satisfy constraints. Truth maintenance systems [Doyle 1977] are also closely related to constraint-satisfaction systems.

A transformation technique with goals similar to constraint satisfaction is narrowing [Hullot 1980]. Narrowing consists of applying the minimal substitution function to a term such that it is reducible, and then reducing (rewriting) it in one step. Thus narrowing does a full unification between the head of a rewrite rule and the term to be narrowed before each rewriting, rather than the simple pattern matching done in term rewriting. Narrowing has recently been used as an operational semantics for logic programming languages [Dershowitz 1985]. An advantage of narrowing is that, like logic-programming languages, it can use searching techniques to explore multiple solutions. The generality of narrowing makes it computationally too expensive to be considered as a general-purpose constraint-satisfaction technique. It is also better suited to solving problems containing variables that range over discrete domains, rather than the continuous domains of linear equations.

2.2 Higher-Order Constraints

A major factor in determining the power of a constraint-satisfaction system will be whether it can handle **second-order constraints** — constraints on other constraints. An example of a second-order constraint is

```
if x = y then b = c/a
```

This if/then constraint takes a predicate and a first-order constraint as an argument to make a new constraint. Second-order constraints can be treated as a Boolean combination of first-order constraints, and solved as a single (larger) constraint, assuming our constraint-satisfaction system is powerful enough to handle Boolean expressions. Other higher-order constraints can resemble higher-order functions in functional languages, such as the *map* function, which takes a scalar constraint and maps it onto a list of scalars.

There has been some confusion between higher-order constraints and meta-constraints. **Meta-constraints** are constraints on the constraint-satisfaction mechanism, and might be used to specify the accuracy required by a relaxation algorithm (and thus the number of iterations required), or even the conditions under which relaxation might be used to solve a problem. Meta-constraints will not be discussed further in this book.

2.3 Constraints Involving Time

Constraint satisfaction usually deals with assertions that are time independent. In the examples above, a constraint such as $a = 0$ means that a is *always* equal to zero.

Many problems are not independent of time; they involve constraints between time and other objects. For example, in an animation we might want to constrain the position of some object as a function of time. In this example, time is an independent variable whose value is supplied from outside the constraint system (by a clock). Values inside the constraint system can depend on the value of time, but not vice versa. In the most general case, however, time must be treated as a fully constrainable object. For example, in the same animation, if we know the velocity of the object (as a function of time) and what position we want it to be in at some time in the future, the constraint-satisfaction system should be able to calculate its position in time by working backwards from its terminal position.

Retraction

Solving constraints involving time can be very difficult, but dealing with constraints that change only as a function of time is somewhat easier. A closely related problem is dealing with constraints that might change, even if they are not explicitly dependent on time. For example, the user might decide that a is *not* equal to zero, delete that constraint, and set it equal to something else. If it is only the value of an object that changes (and not the topology of the constraint graph), such changes can be handled with a form of propagation called **retraction**. Retraction works by propagating changes through the constraint graph. To propagate a change, we *retract* the old value (set its value to *unknown*), which may retract other values that were calculated from this value, and then propagate the new values.

Retraction can also work for values that change as a function of time (where time is an independent variable). The constraints are solved as if they are time invariant, and then, for each new (discrete) value of time, we retract the old value and propagate the new one. In an animation, for example, we would do this for each discrete frame of output. Alternatively, a certain value could be set up to change automatically as a function of time. For example, we could read the position of a mouse or other graphic input device at some regular interval and position some graphic object based on that value. Or the mouse could be used to point to a value on one of several graphically displayed thermometers, one for each temperature-measurement system. Using retraction, the constraint system could repeatedly calculate the equivalent temperatures and display them on the other thermometers.

Retraction as a mechanism for handling change has been fairly popular in constraint-satisfaction systems that use local propagation since it is easy to propagate changes, but it has a number of problems. For example, consider again the temperature-conversion program. If we assign zero to the variable F, and propagate as before, the graph will look like Figure 2.15.

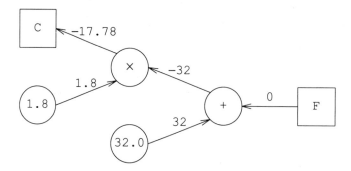

Figure 2.15   The Celsius value of 0 degrees Fahrenheit

Now, let us change the constant 32.0 to 491.67, as in Figure 2.16. For simplicity, instead of retracting old values and then propagating new values, this example will only propagate changes. In general we cannot do this since it might result in a value remaining known when it should have been retracted, such as a value that was known because of a multiplication by zero.

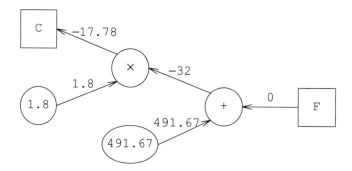

Figure 2.16   The constant 32 changed to 491.67

There is now a contradiction at the plus node, since −32 plus 491.67 is not zero. The plus node has three arcs, so we have three choices of what to change. We cannot change its lower input arc, since 491.67 is a constant. Our next option is to change the value on its upper input arc from −32 to −491.67. Since 1.8 is a constant, this would result in C being changed to −273.15. Our last option is to change the value of F to 459.67.

Changing a value in a graph will almost always result in a change to one or more of our original premises, in this example either C or F. Knowing which value to change is a difficult problem since it depends on what the user intended to happen, something that cannot be determined automatically. There are a number of methods for dealing with this problem:

- Pick the premises that cause the least change in the rest of the graph. This solution may require changing each set of premises in turn, and determining which resulted in the least number of propagations. It can still do the "wrong" (unexpected) thing, such as in the example above, where the user's intent may have been to calculate the Celsius value of absolute zero.

- Pick the premises that are closest to the change (the variable F above). This solution is cheaper than the option above, but is more often "wrong."

- Make the user specify which premises to change. This can be confusing to the user, especially if the user does not know which premises he or she wanted to change.

- Pick some premises, even at random, but allow the user to complain if the choice was "wrong." This is the solution used by many constraint-satisfaction systems.

   If a constraint-satisfaction system uses defaults (see the next section), then they should be changed before other premises, but the system still needs to pick between the different defaults. If the system runs out of defaults to change, then it still must have some mechanism for picking which premises to change.

   Besides the problem of trying to guess the user's intentions when picking which premises to change, retraction also has a number of other problems. Retraction will often result in the needless retraction and recalculation of variables whose values are not affected by the change. In addition, as mentioned above, retraction can only deal with values that change, not with changes in the topology of the constraint graph.

   A similar technique that overcomes some of the problems of retraction has been used by systems that use local propagation of degrees of freedom. If a value is going to change frequently, perhaps as a function of time, then the final propagation step can be precompiled into a one-step deduction from the value that changes to the values that are dependent on that value. Then each change of the value involves only executing a precompiled function to resatisfy the constraints, not a full retraction-and-propagation step.

   The solutions discussed above regard time as an outside variable, somehow different from the other, normal, variables in a constraint program, and severely restrict the kinds of constraints in which it can be used. Recall from above the animation system in which we know where a graphic object must end up at a certain time, and what its velocity is (as a function of time). A system that uses retraction and regards time as an outside variable could not solve this problem without outside assistance.

2.4 Default Values

A problem that is related to how to deal with values that change over time is how to deal with default values. A **default** value is a value assigned to an object if no other value will ever be assigned to that object. Unless retraction is used, this requires global knowledge of the dependencies between variables. The problem is further compounded by having many different objects with default values. The defaults given to two objects may conflict with each other.

A problem with defaults is that they can lead to trivial solutions to constraint problems. For example, if we ask a graphics-constraint system to draw a four-sided object whose opposite sides are parallel and of equal length (a square), and the default position for points is the origin, then the solution we are likely to get is four points at the origin. To avoid this collapse we need some way to say that unless two points are explicitly constrained to be equal to each other, then they are not to be defaulted equal to each other. A statement such as this is called a **negative** or **implicit default** [Pavlidis 1985].

2.5 Summary

Constraint languages use one or more problem-solving methods, called constraint-satisfaction techniques, to help the user solve problems. Because they are used in the context of programming languages (albeit up until now special-purpose languages), efficiency of execution is of primary importance. Thus the spectrum of constraint-satisfaction techniques trades off between generality and speed. A further consideration is ease of implementation — constraint-satisfaction systems are already difficult enough to build. A particular technique might be eschewed because it is too difficult to implement, or because it is not easily integrated with other techniques used by the language.

Local propagation has been very popular in constraint languages, mainly because it is intuitive and easy to implement, but also because it is fast. Systems that use local propagation are also able to separate the rules for satisfying local constraints from the propagation mechanism, and thus can easily be extended with new rules. Unfortunately, local propagation is extremely limited because it can only consider the values impinging on a single node in the constraint graph. Graphs containing cycles, such as are easily introduced by simultaneous equations, cannot be solved at all, unless the user supplies a redundant view.

Local propagation of degrees of freedom is a slightly less powerful variation of local propagation that can be used to compile constraint graphs into functions; these functions can then be further compiled using traditional techniques. This allows very efficient execution, especially because the compiled constraints can be used repeatedly without re-solving them.

Relaxation can be used to solve many constraint graphs containing cycles, but only at run time, so it cannot be used as a compilation technique. It is also very slow, can only deal with numeric constraints, and works only in special cases. For problems with multiple solutions, relaxation will arbitrarily find one of the solutions. This can be a feature when dealing with underconstrained problems, but can also give a procedural semantics to a constraint language since the solution returned may depend upon the order in which the constraints are solved. Nevertheless, relaxation has been widely used, again, mainly because it is relatively easy to implement.

Graph transformation, also called term rewriting, is more powerful than local propagation because subgraphs larger than a single node can be considered. This allows graphs containing small cycles to be solved (such as $X + X = 6$), which cannot be solved by local propagation. Larger cycles, such as those introduced by simultaneous equations, still cannot be solved by traditional graph-transformation techniques. Graph transformation can be as fast as local propagation and can be used as a compilation technique, but it is more difficult to implement so it has not been commonly used in existing constraint-satisfaction systems. A unique benefit of graph transformation is that it can be used on higher-order constraints.

Equation solvers can solve many constraint programs containing cycles, such as those introduced by linear simultaneous equations, and some forms of nonlinear equations. Equation solvers, however, are very difficult to implement, and even harder to modify, and tend to be slow. Some equation-solving algorithms, such as the one discussed in Section 2.1.7, are as fast as local propagation and have been used in constraint languages, but they are limited in power. Equation solving could be used for compilation, but this has never been done.

None of the constraint-satisfaction techniques discussed above are *general-purpose*, in the sense that they can be used to compute arbitrary computable functions. This has limited constraint languages to specific applications. Some constraint languages implemented on top of extensible languages (such as LISP or Smalltalk) have made the facilities of the implementation language available to the user, but these facilities have not been integrated cleanly with the constraint-satisfaction mechanism.

Of the constraint-satisfaction techniques discussed above, only local propagation and graph transformation allow the problem-solving rules to be separated from the control mechanism. Separating the rules from the control mechanism is important for several reasons. If new rules are easy to add, then the constraint language is *extensible*— allowing new data types and new constraints to be defined without having to modify the control mechanism. The ability to define new data types and functions is an important component of modern general-purpose programming languages. Similar functionality would be required of a general-purpose constraint language.

Separating the rules from the control mechanism also opens up the possibility that a constraint language could be constructed mechanically by a *constraint-language generator*, much like parsers are constructed mechanically from grammar rules. If this were possible, it would make constraint-satisfaction systems much easier to implement and modify.

What is needed is a constraint-satisfaction technique that is *fast*, can be used for *compilation*, and can solve constraint programs containing cycles. It should be *extensible*, allowing new types of objects and new types of constraints between these objects to be defined. In order to solve these new constraints, this technique must be *general* (able to compute any computable function). The user should be able to describe a constraint problem, using data types and constraints appropriate to the problem, and work with the constraint system, by giving it rules for solving sub-problems, until the entire problem is solved.

Chapter 3

Augmented Term Rewriting

Augmented term rewriting is a new inference mechanism that is an extension of standard term rewriting using rewrite rules. Augmented term rewriting adds a name space to standard term rewriting that allows the single assignment of values to variables. It also allows these variables to have types, and to be organized into a hierarchy. These extensions make augmented term rewriting expressive enough so that it can be used for general constraint satisfaction, while retaining most of the advantages of standard term rewriting.

3.1 Term Rewriting

Term rewriting is the application of a set of rewrite rules to an expression to transform it into another expression. The expression to be rewritten is called the **subject expression**. Each **rewrite rule** is an ordered pair of expressions, which we will write as

```
head { body }
```

In the literature, rewrite rules have been written as equations "lhs = rhs," and term rewriting called **equational programming** [O'Donnell 1985]. The left-hand side (lhs) of these equations corresponds to the head of our rewrite rules, and the right-hand side (rhs) to the body.

To apply a set of rewrite rules R to a subject expression E, we find a subexpression S of E that matches the head of a rule R_k in R. The expressions (head and body) of a rewrite rule may contain variables. The head of a rule R_k **matches** an expression S if there is a substitution function φ for the variables in the head of R_k that make it identical to S. When such a match is found, the same substitution function φ is applied to the body of R_k and the resulting expression replaces S in E to produce a new subject expression. This is called **instantiating the rule**.

For example, the head of the rule

```
X + 0 { X }
```

where X is a variable, matches a subexpression of

```
((5 − 3) + 0) × 2
```

namely the subexpression $((5-3)+0)$, where φ substitutes $5-3$ for X. The same substitution function is applied to the body of the rule, and the resulting expression is replaced as a subexpression of the original expression. The new subject expression is

```
(5 - 3) × 2
```

Rewriting is done repeatedly, producing a (possibly infinite) sequence of subject expressions:

$$E_0 \rightarrow E_1 \rightarrow E_2 \rightarrow \ ...$$

Because rewrite rules are often used to reduce expressions to a simpler form, each individual rewriting is called a **reduction**, and a subexpression S that matches the head of a rule is called a **redex** (**red**ucible **ex**pression). If a subject expression does not contain any redexes, it is **irreducible**. The sequence of rewritings terminates if some subject expression E_n is irreducible.

In order for term rewriting to be meaningful there must be some *similarity relation* between the head and body of the rules. This relation is typically equality, as in the example above, but it could be any transitive relation, such as implication, or double implication (if and only if). Thus while rules such as 1 { 2 } are perfectly legal and there is nothing to prevent a user from writing such a rule, they are not very meaningful.

If a set of rewrite rules obeys some similarity relation then these rules can be used to make statements about expressions. For example, by ignoring the fact that rules are *directed* pairs of expressions and allowing rewritings with body { head } as well as head { body }, if some expression E_j can be rewritten into another expression E_k, then E_j and E_k are said to be **similar** with respect to the set of rules. If the similarity relation of the set of rules is transitive and symmetric, then E_j and E_k are also related by the similarity relation. For example, if the similarity relation is equality, then E_j and E_k are equal.

Restrictions on Rewrite Rules

Note that when matching the head of a rule to a redex, the substitution function φ was only applied to the head of the rule, and not to the redex (as in general unification, where the substitution function φ must be applied to both). In order to be able to unify a redex with another expression without applying a substitution function to it, we must ensure that the subject expression does not contain any variables. We do this by requiring that the subject expression be initially variable-free. We also restrict the rewrite rules so that a variable that appears in the body of a rule must also appear in the head. For example, the rule

```
0 { 0 × X }
```

is illegal. This guarantees that we will not introduce any variables into the subject expression. Since the subject expression cannot contain any variables, the substitution function (φ) need not be applied to any redexes in the subject expression. These restrictions allow a greatly simplified form of unification called **one-way matching**.

If the additional restriction is made that each variable in the head of a rule is distinct, then each variable can match a subexpression without regard to the value or structure of the subexpression. This restriction allows an even simpler form of unification called **pattern matching** to be used to match the heads of rules (called patterns) against redexes.

For an expression E, there may be more than one rule whose head matches a subexpression of E. When there is more than one redex, there is a choice as to which one to rewrite first. The order in which we perform rewrites might cause a different expression to be produced, or might even cause the rewriting to fail to terminate. We can solve this problem by observing the following restrictions on rules.

- If the head of two different rules matches the same expression, then the body of these rules must be similar. For example, the rules

```
f(X, 1) { 1 }
f(0, X) { 0 }
```

are illegal since f(0,1) could be replaced by either 0 or 1. In the case where the similarity relation of a set of rules is transitive, this implies no added restriction since the two rules above (assuming the similarity relation is equality) would imply that 1 and 0 are equal.

- When the head of two (not necessarily different) rules match two different subexpressions, the two subexpressions must not overlap (match different but non-disjoint parts of the same subexpression). For example, the rules

```
f(g(X)) { p }
g(h(X)) { q }
```

are illegal, since they overlap in f(g(h(0))). This restriction keeps the sequence of rewritings from diverging. If these two rules were allowed, then the expression f(g(h(0))) could be rewritten into either p or f(q).

O'Donnell showed that with these restrictions, any order of rewriting that eventually rewrites all outermost redexes will be **confluent** — it will produce the *same* irreducible expression from a given expression, if it exists [O'Donnell 1977]. If the similarity relation of a set of rules is transitive then the irreducible expression resulting from rewriting an expression is called its **normal form**. If an expression has no normal form (the rewritings do not terminate), then its normal form is undefined (equal to **bottom**). If the similarity relation is equality, then the original expression is equal to bottom. The restriction on the order of evaluation that all outermost redexes eventually be rewritten means that our term rewriting system is not bottom preserving. For example, the rules

```
g(X) { g(g(X)) }
f(X,0) { 0 }
```

make the expression g(0) equal to bottom, but the expression f(g(0),0) equal to 0.

From now on, we will assume (unless otherwise noted) that rule sets meet all of the restrictions above, and that their similarity relation is equality (including logical equivalence).

3.1.1 Algebra and Arithmetic

One common application of rewrite rules is to reduce expressions to normal form using rules from some algebra. Typical rules might be

```
~ ( ~ (X)) { X }
X × 1 { X }
X × 0 { 0 }
X + 0 { X }
```

where ~ is the Boolean "not" operator. We can also use rewrite rules to do numeric computations. For example, if we take the last two rules above, and add the following two recursive rules, they form the definitions of the integer arithmetic functions addition and multiplication, where s(X) represents the integer successor of X.

```
X + s(Y) { s(X + Y) }
X × s(Y) { X×Y + X }
```

Of course, an implementation of an algebraic simplification system using term rewriting would not actually perform arithmetic this way. Instead, for efficiency, we would use the machine-language instructions for addition and multiplication.

One limitation of using the recursive definitions for arithmetic is that they do not let us model arithmetic exception conditions. Instead, let us define arithmetic using rules such as

```
1 + 1 { 2 }
1 + 2 { 3 }
```
and so on ...

There would be a very large number of these rules, so we would never actually write them all out. As before, we would use machine instructions, but now we can model arithmetic exception conditions. For example, we do not include a rule for a division by zero, which means that the term n/0 is in normal form. This allows us to deal with infinite values in a uniform manner, including applying transcendental functions to them. For example, we can define a rule to rewrite the arctangent of $n/0$ to $\pi/2$ for positive n. Any other division by zero would remain in normal form, or we can explicitly define a rule that rewrites a division by zero into an error message.

Similarly, since we are really using machine-language instructions to perform arithmetic, we do not include rules to compute the sum of two numbers that would cause a machine overflow. This allows us to define additional rules (perhaps recursively as above) that perform arithmetic on multiples of the biggest number our machine instructions can handle. Thus the efficient machine instructions can be used for normal arithmetic, but recursively defined rules for arithmetic on big numbers would be used automatically if the machine instruction would have overflowed.

3.1.2 The Purdue Equational Interpreter

The Purdue Equational Interpreter is a term-rewriting system for rules whose similarity relation is equality. This language can be used directly as a programming language, and has also been used to implement interpreters for other languages, including LISP and Lucid. It shares with other term-rewriting systems a simple, declarative semantics based on logical consequences of equational theories.

The equational interpreter uses a fast pattern-matching algorithm whose speed is linear in the size of the subject expression and independent of the number of rules. In order to use this algorithm we must place an additional restriction on our rules, called *strict left-sequentiality* [Hoffmann 1985] (also discussed in Section 7.1.1). There is a way to remove this restriction that still results in the same time complexity for rules that are strictly left-sequential, but is of higher order for rules that are not left-sequential.

A program in this language is of the form

```
Symbols
    symdes₁;
    ...
    symdesₙ.
For all var₁, var₂, ... :
    eqn₁;
    ...
    eqnₘ.
```

The symbol descriptors list the symbols of the language to be defined and give their arity. Symbols of zero arity are constants, and symbols of higher arity are operators. Variables are explicitly declared, and the rules are equations of the form lhs = rhs.

An interesting feature of the equational interpreter is that the expressions used in the equations have no fixed syntax. The programmer can choose between several predefined syntaxes, including a standard mathematical functional prefix notation and a LISP-style notation, or even create a new one.

In order to avoid having to list out all numeric constants there are a number of predefined symbol classes, including `integer_numerals`, `truth_values`, `character_strings`, and `atomic_symbols`. These symbol classes have corresponding predefined classes of equations that implement the standard operations on them. The only operation on `atomic_symbols` is a test for equality.

Even with the predefined equations there will be cases where the set of equations the user wants is much too large to type in. To get around this problem, the equational interpreter allows qualifications on the syntactic *class* of a symbol. For example, a predicate to indicate whether an object is an atom (as opposed to a list constructed using *cons*) could be defined as

```
For all x, y :
atom (cons(x, y)) = false;
atom(x) = true  where x is either
        in atomic_symbols
        or in integer_numerals.
```

Unfortunately this feature is limited to the predefined symbol classes. It would be desirable to be able to define new classes of symbols so a single equation could operate on all symbols of that class, instead of having to use a separate equation for each one. For example, we could define a new symbol class `color`, whose elements are `red`, `green`, `yellow`, `blue`, and so on.

Term Rewriting Example

A powerful feature of the equational interpreter that is a consequence of its use of term rewriting is its ability to define and use infinite data structures, which is similar to the use of nonstrict operators in LISP. The following example [from O'Donnell 1985], is in the equational interpreter's LISP.M notation, where function application is denoted by `function[arg1;arg2]`, and `(a.b)` is a special notation for the list constructor `cons[a;b]`. It defines the nullary function `primes` that returns an infinite list of all the prime numbers.

```
Symbols
    /* list manipulation, logical, and arithmetic operators */
    cons: 2;
    nil: 0;
    first, tail: 1;
    firstn: 2;
```

```
    cond: 3;
    add, multiply, modulo, equ, less: 2;
    /* operators for prime sieve */
    intlist: 1;
    sieve: 2;
    factor: 2;
    primes: 0;
    include integer_numerals, truth_values.
For all i, j, q, r:
    /* return the head of a list */
    first[(i . q)] = i;
    /* return the tail of a list */
    tail[(i . q)] = q;
    /* return the first i elements of a list */
    firstn[i ; q] = cond[ equ[i; 0]; ();
        (first[q] . firstn[ subtract[i; 1]; tail[q] ] )];
    /* standard conditional */
    cond[true; i; j ] = i;  cond[false; i; j ] = j;
    include addint, multint, modint, equint, lessint;
    /* generate infinite list of integers beginning with i */
    intlist[i] = (i . intlist[ add[i; 1] ] );

    /* sieve[p; r] is all p that are not multiples of any r */
    sieve[(i . q); r] = cond[ factor[i; r];
        sieve[q; r]; (i . sieve[q; r] )];
    /* factor[i; r] is true if r contains a factor of i */
    factor[i; (j . r)] = cond[ less[i; multiply[j; j ] ]; false;
        cond[ equ[ modulo[i; j ]; 0]; true; factor[i; r] ] ];
    /* primes[ ] is the infinite list of prime numbers */
    primes[ ] = (2 . sieve[ intlist[3]; primes[] ] ).
```

This example also shows how to define rules for conditionals and list manipulation operators. The actual primes program consists of the last three rules.

The equational interpreter is based on equational logic, which is less expressive than logics such as the Horn-clause logic used by Prolog. The advantage of using equational logic is that programs can be specified purely declaratively. Interpreters for Prolog cannot find all logical consequences of a program, or waste time searching through irrelevant branches of a search tree, unless control mechanisms such as the cut operator are used. Unfortunately, these control mechanisms give Prolog a procedural semantics. The equational interpreter will "always discover all of the logical consequences of a program, and avoid searching irrelevant ones except in cases that inherently require parallel computation" [O'Donnell 1985, p. 3].

3.2 Augmented Term Rewriting

While term-rewriting systems based on equational logic can be used for algebraic simplification, they are not expressive enough to simplify simultaneous equations directly. In order to use term rewriting as a constraint-satisfaction mechanism that can handle general constraint programs (including programs containing cycles), a more expressive logical basis is required. It also was required that the declarative semantics of constraint languages be retained, so the logical basis chosen would have to be able to be implemented efficiently without the use of any procedural control mechanisms.

For these reasons I decided to start with term rewriting based on equational logic, and augment it to make it expressive enough to handle more general constraint programs. A prime consideration was that these extensions not destroy the nonprocedural semantics of term rewriting. In the remainder of this chapter, we will assume that we have a standard term-rewriting system with a set of rules to perform algebraic simplifications. We will then augment this system so that it can be used for constraint satisfaction, including simultaneous equations.

Since term-rewriting systems perform rewritings on a single subject expression, and simultaneous equations are represented as a set of equations, we need some way to treat a set of equations as a single expression. The solution to this problem is to treat all symbols in the language (including the equal sign) as operators. An interesting benefit of treating the equal sign as an operator is that we can now use it "both ways." Consider the addition operator (+). If the value of the expression

$$x\ +\ 4$$

is known to be 7, then the value of x can be deduced to be 3. Or, instead, if it is known that the value of x is 12, then the value of the expression above can be deduced to be 16. Likewise, we treat the equal sign as a Boolean-valued operator. Consequently, if the value of the expression

$$x\ =\ 4$$

is true, then the value of x can be deduced to be 4. Or, instead, if the value of x is known to be 12, then we can deduce that the value of the expression is false. Thus we can use the equal-sign operator either to assert that two values are equal, or to ask if two values are equal.

A problem occurs because we have no way to indicate the value of a subexpression involving the equal-sign operator. If we use another equal sign, as in

$$(x\ =\ 4)\ =\ true$$

we still need a way to express the value of the second equal sign, and so on, ad infinitum. We solve this problem by introducing the semicolon operator (;). By convention, the right-associative semicolon operator is used to assert that its left argument is true; its value is the value of its right argument. For example, if we want to solve the following two simultaneous equations for the value of y:

```
x = y + 5
x = y × 2
```

we would ask the system for the value of the following expression:

```
x = y + 5 ; x = y × 2 ; y
```

The semicolon is right-associative, and has lower precedence than any other operator, so this is parsed as

```
(x = (y + 5)) ; ((x = (y × 2)) ; y)
```

This expression can be read as "what is the value of y, given that $x = y + 5$, and $x = y \times 2$." Note that the order of equations asserted by the semicolon operator is not important.

To our algebraic simplification rules we also will need to add a few rules for the equal sign and semicolon. For example, the semicolon operator has a left identity of *true*:

```
true ; X { X }
```

Note that the semicolon operator must have a right argument, so if we simply want to assert something we still must supply a (dummy) right argument. If this extra verbiage is undesirable, we can add a rule to make it unnecessary:

```
A ; { A ; true }
```

The unary postfix semicolon operator asserts its left (only) argument, by rewriting it to an infix semicolon operator, with a right argument of true.

Note that in the discussion above we have been talking about the equal sign and semicolon as if they had some intrinsic meaning. These meanings are only conventions, of course, and we can define rules to give any meaning to any operator we please. It would be very confusing to users, however, if the standard conventions were not followed. The point is that the equal sign and semicolon are no different from any other operator, including the plus sign (+), or even the primes operator defined in the last section.

The semicolon operator is similar to the "where" clause used in some equational languages [Jayaraman 1986]. For example, we could rewrite the above example as

```
(y where
        x = y + 5
    & x = y × 2)
```

The user is free to add any desired syntax; adding "where" clauses requires only a single rule:

```
V where E { E ; V }
```

3.2.1 Binding Values to Atoms

The major extension we will make to term rewriting is to allow a limited form of non-local sideeffects — the binding of a value to an atom. First, we must distinguish some atoms as bindable. Using the conventions of traditional languages, for bindable atoms we use names such as `x` or `height`, while nonbindable atoms are strings (enclosed in double quotes) and operators. The numeric constants and the constant atoms such as `true`, `false`, and `nil`, are considered nullary operators.

Binding is done with a special infix operator `is`, whose left argument must be a bindable atom, and whose right argument is an arbitrary expression. The `is` operator rewrites to the constant `true`, and also binds its right argument as the value of its left argument. This binding has a nonlocal sideeffect in that all other occurrences in the subject expression of the newly bound atom name will be replaced by the atom's value. The only restriction is that we must never attempt to bind another value to an atom that is already bound, so that bindable atoms will obey single-assignment semantics.

The ability to bind values to atoms allows us to solve simultaneous equations. For example, consider again the subject expression for the simultaneous equations from the previous section:

```
x = y + 5 ; x = y × 2 ; y
```

We can rewrite the first equation to

```
x is y + 5
```

which then rewrites to `true`, and binds the value $y + 5$ to `x`. We now replace every instance of the atom `x` with $y + 5$, yielding the following subject expression:

```
true ; y + 5 = y × 2 ; y
```

The remaining equation can now be simplified using standard algebraic simplification rules and then solved (using the `is` operator) for the value of `y`. The subject expression is now

```
true ; true ; 5
```

The nullary true operators are then rewritten away using the rule introduced in the last section, leaving the constant 5, which is the desired value of y.

Binding Treated as Adding Rules

An alternative way to visualize binding that ties this concept in tighter with term rewriting is to treat the binding of a value to an atom as equivalent to introducing a new rewrite rule to the system. For example, in the example above, the value $y + 5$ was bound to x. This can be thought of as adding the rule

```
x { y + 5 }
```

to the set of rewrite rules, where x is treated as an atom (not as a variable) by the pattern matcher. These added rules must obey the same restrictions as the existing rules. For example, their heads cannot overlap, which prohibits binding two different values to the same atom name. The added rules must also have the same similarity relation as the existing rules, in this case, equality. We guarantee this by creating expressions containing the is operator only from equations asserted with a semicolon.

A standard term-rewriting system has only a single type of redex — those subexpressions that match the head of some rule. Adding binding to a term-rewriting system means that we now have three possible types of redexes:

- Those subexpressions whose root operator is the is operator. These redexes are rewritten to the constant true, and have the side effect of binding a value to an atom.

- Those atoms that have been bound (that match one of the added rules). These redexes rewrite to the (bound) value of the atom.

- The normal redexes (from standard term rewriting) that match the head of some rule.

If we treat binding as adding rules, however, we must place a restriction on the order of evaluating our rules. Rules introduced by the is operator (the second type, above) must be evaluated before other rules, in particular before we introduce any new instances of the is operator. For example, if x has been bound the value $y + 5$, and the subject expression contains the expression

```
x = 8 ; y
```

then two different rules can match — the added rule for the value of x, and the rule that rewrites the expression above to

```
x is 8 ; y
```

This latter case is illegal since it would try to bind a new value to x. The atom x must be replaced by its value, resulting in the expression

```
y + 5 = 8 ; y
```

and ultimately yielding the value 3 for y.

Of course, we would never implement binding as if new rules were added to the pattern matcher; the full power of a pattern matcher is hardly required to match a single atom name. A simpler implementation would be to keep pointers from each atom name to all occurrences of it in the subject expression, and when a value is bound to an atom, simply replace all occurrences of it by its value before doing any more rule reductions. Nevertheless, we will often discuss the semantics of binding as if new rules were introduced, and, as above, talk about the properties of the added rules.

By making this simple addition to term rewriting we have made it expressive enough to solve simultaneous equations. In fact, in Section 5.1 we will implement the simultaneous-equation solver discussed in Section 2.1.7. We could then use these rules as an equation-solving constraint system.

Variables

In this book, bindable atoms will often be called *variables*, since they behave similarly to variables in traditional programming languages, but it is important to emphasize that they are not variables to the term-rewriting system. When the use of the term *variable* could be confusing the two uses will be differentiated by calling variables to the term-rewriting system **parameter variables** (because they are bound as parameters during pattern matching), and call bindable atoms in the subject expression **free variables** (because they can have a value bound to them by the is operator). Note that these are not the same as free variables in the Lambda Calculus. Furthermore, in this chapter parameter variables will be distinguished from free variables by using upper-case letters for parameter variables, as is common in languages such as Prolog.

Free variables in Bertrand are superficially similar to logical variables in logic programming languages such as Prolog, because values are bound to them as a result of a confluence of constraints. In Prolog this confluence is the result of unification. In augmented term rewriting, however, free variables are treated as atoms to the rewriter; only parameter variables participate in matching and rewriting.

3.2.2 Name Spaces

Now that atoms can have values bound to them, they resemble variables in other programming languages. Thus far, however, the names of these "variables" form a flat name space; in essence they are all global variables. A related problem is that the only objects in our language are primitives such as numbers and Booleans. Most languages allow the programmer to define structured objects that contain sub-objects, like the record data types of Pascal.

In traditional languages these two problems are treated separately, and are solved by introducing two different hierarchies, the hierarchy of variable-name scoping for procedures, and the hierarchy of structured object names. In constraint languages there is no such strong distinction between procedures and data, so we would like to solve both of these problems with the same mechanism. Happily, there is another extension to term rewriting that can solve these problems.

In order to model structured objects in a term-rewriting system, we are going to extend the semantics of rules to allow them to define classes of structured objects. When such an object-constructing rule is reduced, it creates an instance of that class. The names of these structured objects and their sub-objects are organized (as is typical) into a hierarchical name space. We are already using rules as procedures (in the same way that Prolog clauses resemble procedures), so sub-objects are also like local variables of procedures. Thus the same (simple and general) mechanism will be used to add structure to both programs and data.

Labels

First we will tackle the problem of all variable names being global. The problem is that the same name in two different rule invocations can interfere with each other. For example, the rule

```
average(A,B)  { 2 × mean = A + B ; mean }
```

can be used to find the average of two numbers, say 3 and 9, by the following sequence of reductions:

```
average(3,9)
2 × mean = 3 + 9 ; mean
2 × mean = 12 ; mean
mean = 6 ; mean
mean is 6 ; mean
true ; 6
6
```

If we use the `average` rule more than once, as in

        average(3,9) + average(10,20)

both invocations of this rule will introduce instances of the variable `mean`, which will interfere with each other and, in this case, cause a contradiction (note that this is not a problem for parameter variables such as `A` and `B` in the head of the rule).

   To solve this problem, we need a way to keep the free variables of each invocation separate. We do this using **labels**. A label is a bindable-atom (free-variable) name followed by a colon, and is used to label a subexpression of the subject expression. A label is treated as an implied (and optional) parameter to every rule in the term-rewriting system. For example, the rule

        average(A,B) { 2 × mean = A + B ; mean }

is actually treated as if it were written as the rule

        Label : average(A,B) { 2×Label.mean = A+B ; Label.mean }

When a rule is reduced, every free-variable name in the body of the rule is modified by appending its name to the label name, with the two separated by a period. For example if this rule is used to match the expression

        p: average(3,9)

the rewriting produces

        2×p.mean = 3+9 ; p.mean

Different invocations of the same rule can be given different labels, which will keep the free variables from interfering with each other. If a label is omitted, one is assumed. For the purposes of this discussion, we will give these assumed labels names of the form #n, where n is a unique positive integer. Consequently, the expression

        average(3,9) + average(10,20)

rewrites to

   (2 × #1.mean = 3+9 ; #1.mean) + (2×#2.mean = 10+20 ; #2.mean)

which eventually rewrites to the correct answer, 21.

   Note that if we consider a period to be an alphabetical character, the names constructed by concatenating the (possibly generated) label names to the free variable names are still global variables. We get the effect of local variables by using unique label names, but we can still share variables.

Defining New Data Types

As mentioned above, the same solution allows us to create structured objects using rules. We will use labels to name *instances* of these objects. An object-constructing rule defines a class of objects; when the head of this rule matches a subexpression of the subject expression, it creates an instance of this class. If the matched subexpression is labeled, then the label becomes the name of the instance.

We can also create instances of primitive objects (such as numbers) using rules. These objects are like scalar variables in conventional languages. For example, if aNumber is a nullary operator, then

```
aNumber { true }
```

will match a (trivial) subexpression consisting of the nullary operator aNumber and rewrite it to the nullary constant true. For the purpose of this discussion, we will consider this rule to be a *primitive object constructer* that creates an object of type "rational number" as a sideeffect (we will show how this is actually done in Section 3.2.3). For example, the labeled subexpression

```
n: aNumber
```

when reduced, creates an object named n (in the name space) that is an instance of a rational number. The sideeffect of creating a number does not affect normal rule rewriting — the expression above is still rewritten to the constant true.

Now that we have at least one primitive object constructer, we can define other objects using the primitives. For example, if aPoint is a nullary operator, then the rule

```
aPoint { x: aNumber ; y: aNumber ; true }
```

when it matches a redex, creates an object with two sub-objects, both of which are numbers. This object can be thought of as a point, although we do not yet have a way to name types (type names will be introduced in Section 3.2.3). An instance of this pointlike object named p1 can be created by placing the following labeled subexpression in the subject expression:

```
p1: aPoint
```

As above, a useful operational interpretation of the name-space hierarchy is that it is implemented by appending the bindable atom names (including labels) inside the body of the rule to the label of a redex when the rule is instantiated. For example, the labeled redex:

```
p1: aPoint
```

can be thought of as rewriting to

```
p1.x: aNumber ; p1.y: aNumber ; true
```

where the redex label `p1` is concatenated onto the bindable atom names (x and y) in the body of the matched rule. As mentioned above, object names form a hierarchical name space like the name space for record data types in Pascal. For example, the sub-objects of the object `p1` are `p1.x` and `p1.y`.

User-defined objects can be incorporated in other objects, building new structures hierarchically on top of others. For example, the following rule will create an object that can be thought of as a line segment

```
aLine { p: aPoint ; q: aPoint ; true }
```

If our subject expression contains the redex

```
ln: aLine
```

then a single line will be inserted in the name space. This line will have two points as sub-objects, and each point will have two numbers, as shown in Table 3.1.

Table 3.1		
lines	points	numbers
ln		
	ln.p	
		ln.p.x
		ln.p.y
	ln.q	
		ln.q.x
		ln.q.y

In Section 3.1.1 we used rules to define operations on the primitive data types, and now we can use rules to define new operations on our new data types. For example, `horiz` is a prefix operator that is used to constrain a line to be horizontal.

```
horiz L { L.p.y = L.q.y }
```

The `horiz` operator applied to a line, say `ln` (created by the `aLine` operator above):

```
horiz ln ;
```

rewrites to

```
ln.p.y = ln.q.y ;
```

an assertion that the y coordinate of the line's beginning point (p) is equal to the y coordinate of the line's ending point (q). This equation is an assertion because it is the left argument of a semicolon operator. If used without a semicolon, the same `horiz` operator could be used to ask if a line is horizontal.

In order to clarify how these rules work, we will now list the steps that an augmented term-rewriting system might go through in rewriting the following subject expression:

```
ln: aLine ; horiz ln ;
```

The redex about to be reduced will be shown in italics. In this example, we always reduce the leftmost redex, but any other order would be just as valid. For simplicity, redexes of the form

```
true ;
```

are not shown; they are rewritten away as soon as they are created.

```
ln: aLine; horiz ln;
ln.p: aPoint; ln.q: aPoint; horiz ln;
ln.p.x: aNumber; ln.p.y: aNumber; ln.q: aPoint; horiz ln;
ln.p.y: aNumber; ln.q: aPoint; horiz ln;
ln.q: aPoint; horiz ln;
ln.q.x: aNumber; ln.q.y: aNumber; horiz ln;
ln.q.y: aNumber; horiz ln;
horiz ln;
ln.p.y = ln.q.y;
```

At this point we are left with a line, two points, and four numbers, and an assertion that two of the numbers are equal. The `is` operator from Section 3.2.1 could now be used to solve this asserted equation.

Constraints on Data Types

The astute reader may have noticed that all of our object-definition rules have ended with the constant `true`. This trailing constant could simply be omitted by replacing the last infix semicolon operator in the rule with a postfix semicolon operator, but we put it there anyway (as a matter of style) to indicate that there is something else that can go there. So far all of our objects have consisted only of data, with no constraints. But object-constructing rules can have constraints. For example, if we change the rule that defines a point to

```
aPoint2 { x: aNumber ; y: aNumber ; y = 0 }
```

then points created with this rule would be constrained to lie on the x axis. The constant `true` at the end of an object-constructing rule can be thought of as meaning that the (nonexistent) constraints on that object are trivially satisfied.

How do these constraints get enforced? In the `aLine` rule

```
aLine { p: aPoint ; q: aPoint ; true }
```

notice that the `aPoint` operators are followed by semicolons. By following a subexpression by a semicolon, we are *asserting* it. The redex

```
p: aPoint ; ...
```

gets rewritten to

```
(p.x: aNumber ; p.y: aNumber ; true) ; ...
```

where the semicolon following the closing parenthesis is the same semicolon that followed the `aPoint` operator. Since the value of the right-associative semicolon operator is the value of its right argument, the value of the expression in parentheses is just `true`. Consequently, the expression above is equivalent to

```
p.x: aNumber ; p.y: aNumber ; true ; ...
```

and the rule

```
true ; A { A }
```

eliminates the redundant expression, leaving

```
p.x: aNumber ; p.y: aNumber ; ...
```

If instead, the rule for `aPoint2` were used instead of `aPoint`, then the subject expression would end up as

```
p.x: aNumber ; p.y: aNumber ; p.y = 0 ; ...
```

and the constraint on the y value of the point would be asserted.

We defined an operator `horiz` above to constrain lines to be horizontal. Instead of creating some lines and then constraining them to be horizontal, we could combine the constraint into the object-constructing rule:

```
aHorizLine { p: aPoint ; q: aPoint ; p.y = q.y }
```

Both methods above are exactly equivalent to adding the same constraint to each line object that we wanted to be horizontal in the subject expression:

```
ln: aLine ; ln.p.y = ln.q.y ;
```

but, using the rules defined above, it is much easier to write, and more meaningful to read, using either of the following two forms:

```
ln: aHorizLine ;
ln: aLine ; horiz ln ;
```

These two forms also have the advantage of being more abstract — the user does not need to know the internal structure of a line in order to constrain it to be horizontal. If lines were defined using polar coordinates, then the rule to make a line horizontal might be defined as

```
horiz L { L.theta = 0 }
```

Thus we can make the internal definition of data types be local to the rules that define and operate on those data types, instead of forcing the user to be concerned with these details.

As discussed above, a rule containing sub-objects can match a redex that is not labeled. In this case, its sub-objects cannot be accessed (from outside the rule) because they cannot be named. For example, if the rule

```
average(A,B) { mean: aNumber ; mean - A = B - mean ; mean }
```

is matched by a redex that is not labeled, then the variable `mean` cannot be named from outside the rule. In this case the object `mean` is acting as a local variable.

Variables and Declarations

Because of their similarity to local variables in traditional programming languages, we will call variable names (bindable atoms such as `mean`) in the body of a rule **local variables**. When a rule containing local variables is instantiated (whether the redex is labeled or not) then the local variables become **free variables** (suitable for binding). Local variables and free variables are really the same thing (they are both bindable atom names), the only difference is whether they are in the body of a rule or instantiated in the subject expression. We distinguish them mainly because it is more natural to refer to the "local variables of a rule," or to the "free variables in a subject expression."

Note that in the last rule for the `average` operator we declared the variable `mean` to be a number. In earlier rules, before we introduced labels and user defined objects, all variables were numbers, so there was no need for declarations. We could make declarations optional for numbers (as in some existing computer languages), but instead, from now on we will require all local variables (including numbers) to be "declared" by using them as the label of an expression that creates an object. This will also help us distinguish names used as operators, such as the `horiz` operator above, from names used as local variables, since all local variables must be declared. In addition, this document will always indicate when an atom name is being used as an operator, and give its arity (and, if important, its precedence).

Primitive objects, such as numbers, strings, and Booleans, can have values bound to them by the `is` operator. Note that user-defined objects, such as the points and lines defined above, are typically not subject to having values bound to them with the `is` operator. Instead, these structured objects have values bound by binding values to their sub-objects. For example, equality over points is defined with the rule

```
p = q { p.x = q.x & p.y = q.y }
```

which says that two points are equal if their x and y components are both equal. Unfortunately, since this rule does not specify that p and q have to be points, the system could also attempt to apply this rule to other objects, such as lines, or even numbers. In order to solve this problem we need some way to distinguish objects of different types from each other. Other languages solve this problem by prohibiting operator overloading, and so require the user to use different operator names (procedure names) for each new data type. As shown in the next section, however, operator overloading is essential in a term-rewriting system.

3.2.3 Types

Types are a general mechanism that replaces the need for syntactic qualifications on the heads of rules, such as the *where* clause in the Purdue Equational Interpreter. The *where* clause was used as a guard on a rule head, so the (parameter) variables of a rule would only match objects of the correct type. For example, we might want a successor operator that only works on integers. Using the syntax of the equational interpreter:

```
succ(N) = N + 1  where N is in integer_numerals
```

the where clause acts as a guard on the type of N.

    The same mechanism is available for an augmented term-rewriting system, but with a different syntax. To distinguish type names from other atom names, types will always begin with a single quote ('). If we assume for the moment that there exists a primitive type of 'integer, then the example above would look like this:

```
succ N'integer { N + 1 }
```

The type name following a parameter variable, such as the variable N above, is called a **guard**.

    We would also like to extend the same mechanism to apply to user-defined classes of objects. For example, we would like the `horiz` operator above to match only parameters that are lines, so that we do not try to make some other data type horizontal by mistake.

```
horiz L'line { L.p.y = L.q.y }
```

All that remains is to be able to attach a type name to an object created by a rule. We do this by placing a type name after an object-constructing rule. For example, the `aLine` and `aPoint` rules become

```
aLine { p: aPoint ; q: aPoint ; true } 'line
aPoint { x: aNumber ; y: aNumber ; true } 'point
```

When the aPoint rule is reduced (for example in the expression p: aPoint from the body of the aLine rule), the label of the redex (p) is inserted into the name space and given the type 'point. A type name placed after a rule body is called a **tag**. It should be noted that the rule above does not define a data type; it is merely a typed object constructer, and there could be (and often will be) many different rules to create objects of the same type.

Another example of a typed object constructor is the rule to create a rational number:

```
aNumber { true } 'number
```

In Section 3.2.2 this rule was treated as a special primitive object constructer, but with types, this rule is no different from any other typed object constructer. When it matches a labeled redex, it "creates" an object (in the name space) of type 'number, which can be used in arithmetic expressions and have arithmetic expressions bound to it as its value by the is operator. We make sure that the is operator only binds values to objects of the correct type by using guards on its arguments, as in any rule.

In the last section, we noted that user-defined types of objects, such as points, are usually not bound values with the is operator. This difference is not due to any special treatment by the language interpreter. What we have been calling user defined objects are simply structured objects, so we naturally define equality on them in terms of the equality of their sub-objects, and do not bind values to them directly. What we have been calling primitive objects are simply objects with no sub-objects, so equality must be defined directly. Unlike most languages, the user is free to introduce new types of "primitive" objects (in the same way that numbers were defined, above), but they are primitive only in the sense that they are atomic.

Supertypes

Type names are organized into a subtype/supertype hierarchy, much like superclasses in object-oriented languages such as Smalltalk. A type name can (optionally) be given a single supertype (how this is done is described in the next section). If type 's is a supertype of type 't, then 't is a subtype of 's, and a guard of type 's will match any object of type 's or type 't. If type 't has any subtypes, then any objects of those types will also match a guard of type 's. Supertypes, like superclasses, are used to organize specific types into more general types.

For example, if 'vehicle is a supertype of 'bicycle, then a parameter with a guard that can match an object of type 'vehicle will also match an object of type 'bicycle. If there are rules that match both a type and its supertype, then the

more specific rule is used. For example, we could define an operator named
`allowed_on_freeway`:

```
allowed_on_freeway X'vehicle { true }
allowed_on_freeway X'bicycle { false }
```

and the more specific (second) rule is used for bicycles, but the first rule is used for
any other vehicle.

Supertypes allow special cases to be handled without resorting to a procedural
semantics, such as trying rules in order as in Prolog. In addition, supertypes can be
implemented as a preprocessing step. The preprocessor makes a copy of each rule for
each subtype, and marks each copy to distinguish it from the original rule. For
example, if `'motorcycle` is also a subtype of `'vehicle`, then the rule

```
allowed_on_freeway X'vehicle { true }
```

is copied to make the following three rules:

```
allowed_on_freeway X'vehicle { true }            (original)
allowed_on_freeway X'motorcycle  { true }        (copy)
allowed_on_freeway X'bicycle { true }            (copy)
```

because `'bicycle` and `'motorcycle` are subtypes of `'vehicle`. Then, when the
rule

```
allowed_on_freeway X'bicycle { false }
```

is preprocessed, it conflicts with an existing rule, but the existing rule is a copy, so
the copy is discarded. The result is the following set of rules:

```
allowed_on_freeway X'vehicle { true }            (original)
allowed_on_freeway X'motorcycle  { true }        (copy)
allowed_on_freeway X'bicycle { false }           (original)
```

The order of the original rules does not matter. If the rule for `'bicycle` was preprocessed first, then, when the rule for `'vehicle` was preprocessed, the copy generated
for `'bicycle` would conflict with an existing original rule, and, again, the copy
would be discarded.

The constant numbers (such as 7 or 42) are treated as a subtype of type `'con-
stant`. Thus in the rules:

```
fact N'constant { N * fact(N-1) }
fact 1 { 1 }
```

the first rule will match any constant, *except* the constant 1, which is matched by the
second rule. Again, the order of the rules does not matter.

Types as Operators

In the examples above, types have mainly been applied to atoms, such as the line `ln`, but some operators, such as the constant numbers, have also behaved as if they were typed. Actually, types are treated as nullary operators, and typing information, such as supertypes, can be applied to any operator. For example, if the nullary operators `true` and `false` are subtypes of type `'boolean`, we can also make the infix operators `>` and `&` be subtypes of `'boolean`, so that expressions such as `a>0 & b>a` will be matched by a rule looking for a `'boolean`.

Currently, types can have at most one supertype, but can have any number of subtypes. Multiple supertypes could be allowed, but might cause problems. For example, if `'bicycle` is a subtype of both `'vehicle` and `'gift`, then the two rules

```
allowed_on_freeway X'vehicle { true }
allowed_on_freeway X'gift { false }
```

would cause a conflict, since an object of type `'bicycle` could match either rule. Of course, this could simply be detected as two conflicting rules, and prohibited. This solution would only define the semantics of multiple supertypes in cases where no conflicts are introduced, and treat all other cases as errors.

Note that our types are not like types in the traditional programming language sense, they are more like guards on statements. Type checking is done at run time and is mainly used for overloading operators (but note that operator overloading, as in the factorial example above, is essential). Bertrand Russell said, "The purpose of type structure is to distinguish those phrases that denote from those that do not denote." We use types in this way; to distinguish those rules that have meaning in a particular situation from those that do not.

3.3 Bertrand

Bertrand is a programming language based on augmented term rewriting that can be used to build constraint-satisfaction systems. This language has been implemented; the remaining examples in this book have all been run on this implementation. This section discusses the differences between Bertrand and the language discussed in the preceding sections.

A minor difference between Bertrand and the language described above is the treatment of the subject expression. In term-rewriting systems the subject expression is separate from the rules. In Bertrand, the subject expression is initially a constant — the nullary operator `main`. The user supplies a (single) rule whose head is the constant `main`, and whose body is the subject expression desired by the user. The local variables of the `main` rule become the free variables of the subject expression.

Another minor difference is that in Bertrand parameter variables are not required to be upper case. Parameter and local (bindable) variables can always be distinguished from each other by the fact that local variables can appear only in the body of a rule, while any parameter variable that occurs in the body must also appear in the head. In addition, local variables must be declared, by using them as a label in the body of the rule.

Another difference is the order of evaluation. In order to guarantee that an answer is produced, if it exists, the restriction was made on the order of evaluation of redexes that all outermost redexes must eventually be rewritten. Unfortunately, this does not guarantee how long it will take to produce the answer. For example, the rules

```
main { f(g(0),0) }
g(X) { g(g(X)) }
f(X,0) { 0 }
```

may validly be rewritten to 0 by applying the second rule one billion times, resulting in the following subject expression:

```
f(g(g(g(g(g(g(g(g( ... )))))))), 0)
```

followed by a single application of the third rule. However, on practical machines (with finite memory) this would result in an error. The undecidability of the halting problem means that we cannot restrict our rules to prohibit infinite (or arbitrarily large) sequences of rewritings without overly restricting the functions that our term-rewriting system can compute. In practice, we must depend on the user to avoid rules such as the first one above, and so in actual implementations of Bertrand we often drop the restriction that outermost redexes be rewritten eventually. This gives us quite a bit of flexibility in choosing our evaluation order. Evaluation order will be discussed further in the Section 3.3.1.

Bertrand also has some slight differences in the name-space hierarchy. The hierarchy introduced in Section 3.2.2 allows access to variables in sub-objects, but not vice versa. Thus a line ln can refer to a sub-object, ln.p, but a point cannot refer to the line it is contained in, or even itself. This type of hierarchy is typically used for structured objects (such as record data types in Pascal), but is different from the scoping rules typically used for local variables. In Pascal, a variable name inside a subroutine refers to the variable defined in the smallest surrounding (possibly global) scope; thus objects (procedures) are allowed to access variables in outer objects.

There is nothing inherent in augmented term rewriting that makes one type of name space preferable to another. We could just as easily have allowed dynamic scoping of variable names, or some other scheme. The scheme chosen, however, has the advantage that it can be used for both local variable scoping and for naming of sub-objects of structured objects, and is thus simpler and more general. It also has a resemblance to the name-space hierarchy of hierarchical file systems, as used in most operating systems.

The hierarchy chosen, however, has *no* global objects, and is very restrictive about what can be referenced from inside an object. To relax this restrictiveness, in Bertrand an object was added at the root of the name-space hierarchy whose name is a single period (.). The root object can be referenced from anywhere in the hierarchy, as can its sub-objects, effectively making them global objects. For example, if we want a line `gline` to be global, we name it `.gline`, and we can then refer to the x coordinate of its beginning point as `.gline.p.x` from inside any rule. This addition allows us to simulate scoping rules such as those used by the C programming language, where variables are either local or global. This scheme is also similar to hierarchical file systems that have a root directory.*

In conventional procedural programming languages, global variables are generally considered bad because their sideeffects can be difficult to trace, they can be hidden by local variables, and they can cause aliasing problems. In Bertrand, all objects (including global objects) must obey single-assignment semantics, so there can be no sideeffects or aliasing effects of any kind. Also, local variables can never hide global variables, since global names are distinct (they begin with a period). Therefore none of the traditional problems with global variables ever arise.

Operator Definitions

Bertrand also must include a way for the user to define new operators and types. Different implementations have handled this in different ways, differing mainly in whether the operator definitions are mixed in with the rules, or are contained in a separate file (or files). For each operator the user must supply its print value and its arity (nullary, unary, or binary). If the operator is unary, it can be prefix, postfix, or outfix.† If the operator is binary, then it is used infix, and can either be left- or right-associative, or nonassociative. Except for nullary and outfix operators, each operator must also have a precedence, which is defined as an integer (higher numbers indicate higher precedence). Operators can optionally have a single supertype. Types are defined similarly to operators. They are assumed to be nullary operators, and can optionally have a single supertype. With the exception of supertype information, operator and type definitions only affect the parser.

---

* It would be interesting to see if an interactive programming environment built around Bertrand could take advantage of this similarity and treat file objects as normal language objects.

† Absolute value (| a |) is an example of an outfix operator, also sometimes called matchfix.

Using a syntax reminiscent of the C preprocessor, here are some typical operator and type definitions:

```
#operator + infix binary left associative precedence 600
#operator - left 600
#operator - prefix precedence 900
#operator begin end outfix
#type 'linear supertype 'expression
#type 'constant supertype 'linear
```

Any blank delimited word that is not a keyword or a number is assumed to be an operator name. The keywords are `nullary`, `unary`, `binary`, `infix`, `prefix`, `postfix`, `outfix`, `matchfix`, `left`, `right`, `non`, `associative`, `nonassociative`, `precedence`, and `supertype`. Any and all keywords are optional, and defaults apply. For example,

```
#operator true
```

defines a nullary operator `true`.

Bertrand is normally used in conjunction with one or more libraries of rules. For example, a library might contain the rules for one or more constraint-satisfaction techniques. Other libraries may contain the basic rules to support some application, such as rules for doing graphics. Several such libraries are developed in Chapters 5 and 6; see also Appendix A for the listings of two libraries — an equation solver and a graphics library. Preprocessor-like statements are also used to include libraries of rules, for example,

```
#include beep.b
```

would include the equation solver.

3.3.1 Evaluation Order

Bertrand inherits many characteristics from term-rewriting systems, including its ability to define recursive rules. Even though Bertrand uses recursion similarly to other languages, it is important to realize that there is no procedural interpretation attached to a recursive definition. For example, consider a factorial function defined as the product of a list of numbers:

```
fact N { prod(ints(N)) }
ints 1 { 1 }
ints A'constant { (ints A-1), A }
prod A'constant { A }
prod (A , B) { (prod A) × (prod B) }
```

A typical interpreter for a language such as LISP or Prolog executes in *applicative order*, and so would run the `ints` rule to completion, producing a list of the first N integers, and then would pass this list to the `prod` rule. Bertrand has no such procedural interpretation of recursion and thus is free to rearrange the order of computation to achieve some goal. A partial trace of the steps that Bertrand uses to calculate the factorial of 8 is

```
(prod (ints 7-1 , 7)) * (prod 8)
(8×7) × ((prod (ints 6-1)) × (prod 6))
(56×6) × ((prod (ints 5-1)) × (prod 5))
(336×5) × ((prod (ints 4-1)) × (prod 4))
(1680×4) × ((prod (ints 3-1)) × (prod 3))
(6720×3) × ((prod (ints 2-1)) × (prod 2))
40320
```

In this case, Bertrand automatically set up a producer/consumer relationship from `ints` through `prod` to the ultimate multiplication, unrolling the calculation enough to keep everything busy. Because the `ints` rule produces its list of values backwards, Bertrand used the commutative and associative laws (expressed as rules) to move the constants to the left so that they can be multiplied together.

Since Bertrand has no prescribed order of evaluation, an interpreter can choose the order with a particular goal in mind. The current implementation of Bertrand tries to minimize the space used by a calculation (constraint programs can sometimes explode), and so attempts to use a value created by a rule before it invokes the same rule again. The trace shown above was executed on a single processor, but it does show how Bertrand exposes potential pipeline concurrency without any effort on the part of the programmer. An implementation of Bertrand on a parallel processor could assign producers and consumers of a list of values to separate processors.

3.3.2 Comparison to Prolog

A general-purpose language that has some similarities to Bertrand is Prolog [Clocksin 1981]. A Prolog program is also a specification that is executable. The relationship between Prolog and Bertrand (or between searching with dependency directed backtracking and augmented term rewriting) is very interesting — while Bertrand is a higher-level language in that it is more descriptive, it is generally less expressive than Prolog. Consider the standard Prolog list append program [Clocksin 1981, p. 55].

```
append([], L, L).
append([X|L1], L2, [X|L3]) :- append(L1, L2, L3).
```

We can ask a Prolog interpreter for the value of X in the following term:

```
append([1,2], [3,4,5], X).
```

and it will answer X = [1,2,3,4,5].

In a standard term-rewriting system, we can write this program using append as an infix operator instead of as a relation:

```
[] append L { L }
[X|L1] append L2 { [X | (L1 append L2)] }
```

We are borrowing the special list notation from Prolog where [] is the empty list, [X|Y] is the list whose head is X and whose tail is Y, and [1,2] is the list cons(1,cons(2,[])).

Our operator notation is somewhat easier to read, but the notation of Prolog is more suggestive of the fact that Prolog deals with relations, not unidirectional functions. Note that even though most Prolog implementations have a mechanism to define operators, it would be difficult to write append as such since, in Prolog, the "value" returned by an operator indicates the success or failure of the operator, not the result of the operation. The arithmetic operators avoid this problem by being evaluated only by the special Prolog is operator.

Since Prolog deals with relations, it can also solve for the value of X in the term

```
append([1,2], X, [1,2,3,4,5]).
```

namely X = [3,4,5]. If we ask a *standard* term-rewriting system the equivalent question:

```
([1,2] append x) = [1,2,3,4,5]
```

it is not powerful enough to solve for the value of x. In order to solve this problem using Bertrand, we restate the problem:

```
([1,2] append x) = [1,2,3,4,5] ; x
```

We then define equality on lists using the rules:

```
[] = [] { true }
[X|L1] = [Y|L2] { X = Y & L1 = L2 }
```

This recursive definition of equality over lists is implicitly built into the unification rules for Prolog, but must be defined explicitly (in a Bertrand library, typically) because Bertrand has no built-in knowledge about equality, over lists or anything else. This is in keeping with the extensible nature of Bertrand, which allows new data types, including lists, to be defined with rules, and then used as if they were primitives. (Actually, in this example only the second rule is necessary.)

These rules then rewrite the problem in the following way:

```
([1,2] append x) = [1,2,3,4,5] ; x
[1, ([2] append x)] = [1,2,3,4,5] ; x
(1=1) & ([2] append x) = [2,3,4,5] ; x
([2] append x) = [2,3,4,5] ; x
[2, ([] append x)] = [2,3,4,5] ; x
(2=2) & ([] append x) = [3,4,5] ; x
([] append x) = [3,4,5] ; x
x = [3,4,5] ; x
```

We can then use the `is` operator to bind the list to the atom x, resulting in

```
true ; [3,4,5]
[3,4,5]
```

Finally, Prolog can even answer questions that look like this:

```
append(X, Y, [1,2,3,4,5]).
```

by generating *sequentially* all the possible values for X and Y, which, when appended together, equal [1,2,3,4,5]. Prolog does this by searching, which adds to the expressiveness of Prolog, but unfortunately, also requires a procedural semantics to keep the execution time and space reasonable. Among other things, this procedural semantics makes it much more difficult to detect or take advantage of parallelism. In Bertrand we would have to write a recursive rule to generate all of the possible values for X and Y. Searching could be added to Bertrand, but it should be done without giving up Bertrand's nonprocedural semantics.

The ability to provide multiple solutions to a problem makes Prolog more expressive than Bertrand, but many aspects of Bertrand are more expressive than Prolog. For example, arithmetic in Prolog is handled using the infix `is` operator. This operator is not invertible, so in order to solve simultaneous equations using Prolog a program would have to be written, while in Bertrand simultaneous equations can be expressed and solved directly. Bertrand also has abstract data types, while in Prolog the user is limited to terms (including lists formed from `cons` terms).

Other languages have extended logic programming to make it more expressive. For example, EQLOG is a language that combines logic programming with term rewriting [Goguen 1984]. This combination would make a very powerful constraint language; unfortunately, it has yet to be implemented, and currently known implementation techniques (based on narrowing) would cause severe execution speed problems. Another possible approach to getting the expressiveness of searching without quite so high a cost would be to use set abstraction techniques with rewrite rules, as in the language EqL [Jayaraman 1986].

Chapter 4

Existing Constraint Languages

This chapter examines existing constraint languages and gives examples of their use. The purpose of this is twofold. Chapters 5 and 6 will describe some constraint-satisfaction systems built using Bertrand to solve the same example problems. We do this primarily to demonstrate that Bertrand can be used to solve constraint-satisfaction problems as well as or better than existing systems. The second purpose of this chapter is to demonstrate the power and usefulness of constraint languages. Proposing a new implementation technique is only meaningful if there is a need for what one is proposing to implement. As there is no existing general survey of constraint languages, and many of the references are difficult to obtain, this chapter will also serve as a survey of existing constraint languages and systems.

Many existing constraint-satisfaction systems have sophisticated, interactive, and often graphical interfaces. On one hand, these interfaces are independent of the issue of constraint satisfaction, and the constraint-satisfaction systems we build with Bertrand will ignore such interface issues. On the other hand, constraint languages lend themselves to such sophisticated interfaces, and it is important to show how existing languages take advantage of this. While such a sophisticated interface has not yet been constructed for Bertrand, it is reasonable to indicate how one might be, so while we are examining existing languages we can at least take a quick look at their interfaces.

Those readers who are familiar with constraint languages can skip over much of the material in this chapter and concentrate only on the examples. Alternatively, this entire chapter can initially be skipped; the sections in Chapters 5 and 6 that build constraint languages to reimplement the examples in this chapter all contain references to the relevant sections here. The reader can then compare the examples directly.

Constraint-satisfaction systems will be classified according to the mechanisms they use. In particular, existing systems fall into one of two categories depending on what method they use to solve constraint programs containing cycles. One group uses numeric techniques such as relaxation to break constraint cycles. The other group uses symbolic techniques to transform constraint programs containing cycles into equivalent programs that do not.

As discussed in Section 2.1, as constraint-satisfaction techniques become more sophisticated, they tend to become more application-specific. Consequently, most existing constraint languages have been written with one or more applications in mind. Existing constraint languages have been used for such things as modeling graphic objects, typesetting graphics, simulating physical laws, building financial models, and solving algebraic problems.

4.1 Constraint Languages That Use Numeric Techniques

The following four systems (Sketchpad, ThingLab, TK!Solver, and Juno) use iterative approximation techniques (typically some form of relaxation) to solve constraint programs containing cycles.

4.1.1 Sketchpad

The Sketchpad system, written by Ivan Sutherland as part of his Ph.D. thesis at M.I.T., "makes it possible for a man and a computer to converse rapidly through the medium of line drawings" [Sutherland 1963, p. 329]. Its use of constraints, sophisticated interactive graphical interface, macro facility, and instancing features were years ahead of its time. Using Sketchpad, a user could draw a complex object by sketching a simple figure and then adding constraints to it.

For example, the steps required to construct a regular hexagon are shown in Figure 4.1. First an arbitrary six-sided polygon is sketched. While sketching, the current line being drawn acts like a "rubber band" between the end of the last line and the cursor position, to give the user immediate feedback. When the cursor approaches an existing point, such as the end of a line, it "snaps" onto it so that closed figures can easily be sketched. Next, to make the polygon regular, the vertices of the polygon are constrained to lie on a circle and to be of equal length. Lastly, the circle used to construct the drawing is deleted, leaving the regular hexagon.

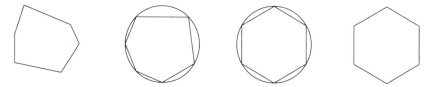

Figure 4.1   Drawing a regular hexagon using Sketchpad

Points, lines and circular arcs are primitive graphical objects in Sketchpad. Any drawing, such as the hexagon above, can be used like a primitive object by turning it into a **macro**. A macro has a set of "attachment points" that are used to merge an instance of it into another drawing.

Primitive constraints include making two lines parallel, perpendicular, or of equal length. Lines can also be made horizontal or vertical, and a point can be constrained to lie on a line or arc. Another constraint type produces a set of digits on the display for some scalar numeric value. Constraints are represented abstractly on the display as a circular node containing a symbol, for example, Figure 4.2 contains the graphical representations of the two constraints to make lines parallel and to make the length of two lines equal.

Figure 4.2   Abstract constraints

The dashed lines connect the constraint to its attachment points. In this case the constraints are not attached to anything, so they are shown attached to a dummy point — indicated by an X.

Constraints are represented internally as error expressions that evaluate to zero when the constraint is satisfied. These constraints are hard-coded into the system, but the macro facility can be used to simulate the addition of new constraints. For example, Figure 4.3 show two lines that are constrained to be parallel and of equal length.

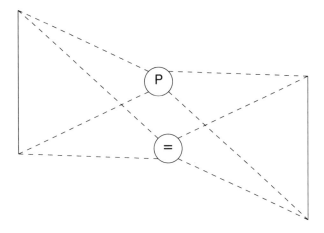

Figure 4.3   Creating a macro

We can use this drawing as a constraint by converting it into a macro with the two lines as attachment points. When we want to use this constraint, we call up an instance of the macro and *merge* the attachment lines with the lines we wish to constrain to be parallel and of equal length.

A **merge** is like a constraint that makes two objects equal, except that the two objects are actually replaced by the equivalent single object. Merges are performed recursively, so that all sub-objects are also merged. For example, when two lines are merged, their endpoints are merged; when two points are merged, their x and y coordinates are merged. Merging two scalar values is a primitive, which makes the two values equal.

Sketchpad satisfies constraints using propagation of degrees of freedom, which Sutherland calls the **one-pass method**. When this method fails, relaxation is used. For the initial values of the relaxation step Sketchpad uses the current values from the drawing on the screen. This, plus the fact that the geometric constraints that Sketchpad uses are fairly well behaved, makes relaxation reasonably fast and interactive.

Unfortunately, Sketchpad used expensive (at that time) graphics input and display hardware. Its interactive mode of operation depended on high-bandwidth communication between the user and the processor, bandwidth that cannot be sustained by batch or time-shared computer systems. The environment to support such a system was very uncommon until personal workstations became economically justifiable. Consequently, Sketchpad was indeed ahead of its time; it was not to be duplicated for over 15 years.

4.1.2 ThingLab

ThingLab is a constraint-based simulation laboratory that builds the power of a Sketchpad-like system on top of the interactive Smalltalk-76 programming environment. It was written by Alan Borning as part of his Ph.D. thesis at Stanford, and originally ran on the Xerox Alto computer, one of the first personal workstations.

In Sketchpad, constraints were uniformly described as error expressions. An early version of ThingLab described constraints this way, and only used relaxation. ThingLab was extended so that constraints could include Smalltalk procedures that give an algorithm for satisfying the constraint. New classes of objects and constraints can be defined, which allows ThingLab to be extended to new domains by a user who can program in Smalltalk. ThingLab's capabilities are still being developed. The most recent version includes the ability to define higher-order constraints [Borning 1985a] and to edit the constraint graphs interactively [Borning 1985b]. The version discussed in the remainder of this section is the version reported on in Borning's thesis [Borning 1979].

In addition to the constraint-satisfaction methods used by Sketchpad, ThingLab also uses propagation of known states. ThingLab gains speed by dividing constraint satisfaction into two stages: planning and run time. During planning, a Smalltalk procedure, called a **method**, is automatically generated for satisfying a set of constraints. This method can then be invoked repeatedly at run time. For example, the corner of a rectangle can be dragged around the screen in near real time and the rectangle will follow; the constraints on the rectangle being satisfied by calling the compiled procedure. If the user changes any constraints, a new method is automatically compiled.

As an example, we will define a set of ThingLab classes that can be used to simulate the connection of common electrical components such as resistors and batteries. This example is a simplified version of an example taken from Borning's thesis [Borning 1979, p. 33]. Borning expects that classes such as these would be defined "by an experienced user of the system." "Using these classes, a less sophisticated user could then employ them in constructing a simulation" [Borning 1979, p. 33]. Simulations are constructed using ThingLab's graphical interface. The end user need not be concerned with the textual class definitions.

In order to use ThingLab's graphical interface, a graphical description would have to be included in the class definitions, along with the electrical description. For the sake of brevity we will ignore the graphical description, which can be quite complex, and concentrate on the electrical description of the components.

Electrical circuits are built up using the class ElectricalLead. An ElectricalLead is the terminal of an electrical component, such as a resistor, and has an associated voltage and current (if represented graphically, it would also have an associated screen location and orientation).

```
Class ElectricalLead
   Superclasses
      ElectricalObject
   Part Descriptions
      voltage: a Voltage
      current: a Current
```

A Ground is an ElectricalLead whose voltage is constrained to be zero.

```
Class Ground
   Superclasses
      ElectricalLead
   Constraints
      voltage = 0.0
         voltage ← 0.0
```

The first line under Constraints yields the error expression for the voltage — the error is zero if the voltage is zero. The second line gives a procedure for satisfying the constraint — set the variable voltage to zero.

A TwoLeadedObject is an abstract class that can be used to define components with two leads. Its constraint is that the current flowing out of one lead must be equal and opposite to the current flowing out of the other lead.

```
Class TwoLeadedObject
   Superclasses
      ElectricalObject
   Part Descriptions
      lead1: an ElectricalLead
      lead2: an ElectricalLead
   Constraints
      lead1 current + lead2 current = 0.0
         lead1 current ← 0.0 - lead2 current
         lead2 current ← 0.0 - lead1 current
```

Note that there are two procedures for satisfying the constraint. The first one can be used to calculate the current through lead1 if we know the current through lead2, or the second one can be used if we know the current through lead1. ThingLab will select the first procedure in order depending on which information is known.

Given the definition of a two-leaded component, the definition of a resistor is fairly straightforward:

```
Class Resistor
   SuperClasses
      TwoLeadedObject
   Part Descriptions
      resistance: a Resistance
   Constraints
      (lead1 voltage - lead2 voltage) = (lead1 current * resistance)
         lead1 voltage ← lead2 voltage + (lead1 current * resistance)
         lead2 voltage ← lead1 voltage - (lead1 current * resistance)
         lead1 current ← (lead1 voltage - lead2 voltage) / resistance
      resistance reference
```

To the constraints on a TwoLeadedObject, class Resistor adds one additional constraint — Ohm's law. In the Ohm's law constraint, the variable resistance has been designated as reference only, so that the system will satisfy the constraint by changing the voltages and currents, not by changing the value of the resistor.

We also define a class for batteries:

```
Class Battery
  Superclasses
    TwoLeadedObject
  Part Descriptions
    internalVoltage: a Voltage
  Constraints
    lead1 voltage = (lead2 voltage + internalVoltage)
      lead1 voltage ← lead2 voltage + internalVoltage
      lead2 voltage ← lead1 voltage - internalVoltage
    internalVoltage reference
```

In order to connect components together in series, we merge the appropriate leads. ThingLab, like Sketchpad, does merges recursively, so merging two leads causes their currents and voltages to be set equal.

We can build a simple voltage divider by connecting a battery and two resistors in series:

```
Class VoltageDivider
  Superclasses
    ElectricalObject
  Part Descriptions
    r1: a Resistor
    r2: a Resistor
    b1: a Battery
    gnd: a Ground
  Merges
    r1 lead2 ≡ r2 lead1
    r2 lead2 ≡ b1 lead1
    b1 lead2 ≡ r1 lead1
    b1 lead1 ≡ gnd
```

A typical use of this simulation might be to set the resistors to be 100 ohms each, the battery to 10 volts, and ask what the current through the circuit is. The resultant circuit, if drawn, might look like Figure 4.4.

Local propagation cannot find a solution to this constraint graph, so relaxation is used. Propagation failed because the current flowing in the circuit depends on the total series resistance, but the constraint satisfier has no way to calculate this resistance directly without knowing the voltage across each resistor, which circularly depends on the current through the resistor. A human problem solver (with knowledge of electrical circuits) would know that the resistance of two resistors in series is the sum of the individual resistors, but our constraint satisfier has no such global knowledge.

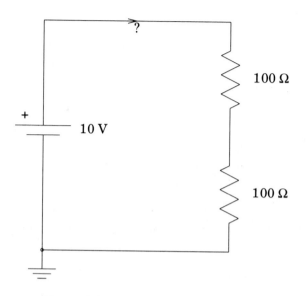

Figure 4.4   An electrical circuit

We can avoid relaxation by supplying the constraint satisfier with a redundant view — another way of looking at two resistors in series.

```
Class SeriesResistors
   Superclasses
      ElectricalObject
   Part Descriptions
      rA: a Resistor
      rB: a Resistor
      rSeries: a Resistor
   Constraints
      rSeries resistance = rA resistance + rB resistance
         rSeries resistance ← rA resistance + rB resistance
         rA resistance reference
         rB resistance reference
   Merges
      rA lead2 ≡ rB lead1
      rA lead1 ≡ rSeries lead1
      rB lead2 ≡ rSeries lead2
```

The user can then graphically merge an object of class SeriesResistors with the two resistors r1 and r2 above, and the system can be solved using local propagation.

A limitation of ThingLab is that in the constraint program on page 76, we had to specify that the resistance of a resistor was a reference value so the system would not change it to satisfy a constraint. This assumes that the user's intention was to specify the values of the resistors and have the system calculate the voltages and currents. Suppose, instead, that the user wanted to have a certain current flowing through a resistor; we should be able to ask the system what value to make a resistor in order to give a certain current flow. Unfortunately, in order to do this the class definition must be modified; something that we did not want the user to be concerned with.

Extensions have been made to ThingLab [Duisberg 1986] to allow it to deal with constraints that are dependent on time. For example, we can build a circuit containing capacitors and inductors, and the system will plot the current versus time. Values of time are supplied from a special variable that cannot be constrained like other (ordinary) variables.

4.1.3 TK!Solver

TK!Solver is "a general purpose problem solving environment" for the IBM PC [Konopasek 1984]. The constraints to be solved are stated to the system as equations. If possible, these equations are solved directly using local propagation (called the **direct solver**), otherwise relaxation is used (called the **iterative solver**). The user must call the iterative solver explicitly by specifying which variables are to be relaxed, and must also provide initial guesses for their values.

The constraint solver is similar to that of ThingLab, except that the user cannot define new objects or constraints. The direct solver can solve simple arithmetic constraints on floating-point numbers, but like other local-propagation techniques it has no knowledge of algebra, so relaxation must be used to solve equations such as $10 = p + p$. If TK!Solver were just an equation solver it would not be very powerful, but it has a number of features that distinguish it from equation solvers.

The user interacts with the system through a number of windows. The equations to be solved are entered into the **rule window**. As each equation is entered, the variables in that equation are automatically entered into the **variable window**, or the user can enter variables explicitly. Each variable in the variable window can either be used for input or output. The user supplies values for input variables, and the system solves for the values of the output variables. If relaxation is to be used, initial guesses must be supplied for each variable to be relaxed. Input variables can be assigned a table of values; the system is solved once for each value in the table, and the results can be graphed using simple line-printer–style graphics. Variables can be given units of measure, such as feet, pounds, or even feet per second, and the system will automatically convert to other units if necessary.

The following example is from "The TK!Solver Book" [Konopasek 1984]. It is given as an example of how to use the system to solve a reasonably difficult word problem. The original problem is a brain teaser from the book *Games for the Super-intelligent* [Fixx 1972].*

> A rope lying over the top of a fence is the same length on each side. It weighs one third of a pound per foot. On one end hangs a monkey holding a banana, and on the other end a weight equal to the weight of the monkey. The banana weighs two ounces per inch. The rope is as long (in feet) as the age of the monkey (in years), and the weight of the monkey (in ounces) is the same as the age of the monkey's mother. The combined age of the monkey and its mother is thirty years. One half of the weight of the monkey, plus the weight of the banana, is one fourth as much as the weight of the weight and the weight of the rope. The monkey's mother is half as old as the monkey will be when it is three times as old as its mother was when she was half as old as the monkey will be when it is as old as its mother will be when she is four times as old as the monkey was when it was twice as old as its mother was when she was one third as old as the monkey was when it was as old as its mother was when she was three times as old as the monkey was when it was one fourth as old as it is now. How long is the banana?

Variable names in TK!Solver refer to numbers and there is no facility for defining data types, so we need to introduce some naming conventions. Each variable name consists of two parts that refer to an object and an attribute of that object, as shown in Table 4.1.

Table 4.1			
Prefix		Suffix	
b	banana	a	age
m	monkey	l	length
M	monkey's mother	w	weight
w	weight	ld	linear density
r	rope		

For example, the variable name rw refers to the weight of the rope, and the name ba would be the age of the banana. Linear density is weight per unit length.

---

*Game by Jim Fixx from GAMES FOR THE SUPER-INTELLIGENT. Copyright © 1972 by James Fixx. Reprinted by permission of Doubleday & Company, Inc.

We enter the information from the problem into the system's rule sheet, as shown in Figure 4.5.

```
                              RULE SHEET
Rule                     Comment
ww = mw                  weight's weight equals monkey's weight
rl = ma                  rope length in feet equals monkey's age in years
mw = Ma                  monkey's weight equals monkey's mother's age
mw/2 + bw =              1/2 monkey's weight, plus banana's weight equals
   (ww + rw)/4           1/4 weight's weight plus rope's weight
Ma = 1/2 *               monkey's mother is 1/2 as old as monkey will be
      3 *                when it is 3 times as old as its Mother,
      1/2 *              when she was 1/2 as old as the monkey will be
                         when it is as old as its mother will be
      4 *                when she is 4 times as old as the monkey was
      2 *                when it was twice as old as its mother was
      1/3 *              when she was 1/3 as old as the monkey was
                         when it was as old as its mother was
      3 *                when she was 3 times as old as the monkey was
      1/4 * ma           when it was 1/4 as old as it is now
```

Figure 4.5   The rule sheet

To finish entering the data from the problem, we supply values for the rope linear density and banana linear density in the variable sheet, and give units to the other variables, as shown in Figure 4.6.

Input	Name	Output	Unit	Comment
		VARIABLE SHEET		
.3333333	rld		lb/ft	rope linear density
	ww		oz	weight of weight
	mw		oz	weight of monkey
2	bld		oz/in	banana linear density
	rl		ft	rope length
	ma		year	age of monkey
	Ma		year	age of monkey's Mother
	bw		oz	weight of banana
	rw		lb	weight of rope
	bl		in	length of banana

Figure 4.6   The variable sheet

At this point we have entered all the information from the problem, but there is additional information that must be supplied. We must supply the conversion factors for our units of measure. This is done in a separate screen called the units sheet, shown in Figure 4.7.

UNITS SHEET		
Convert from	To	Multiply by
ft	in	12
lb	oz	16
lb/ft	in/oz	1.4444444

Figure 4.7   The units sheet

We must also add the definitions for linear density to the rule sheet.

RULE SHEET	
Rule	Comment
bw = bld * bl	definition of banana linear density
rw = rld * rl	definition of rope linear density

Figure 4.8   The rule sheet (continued)

We can now try the direct solver (local propagation) but nothing can be solved because the problem contains simultaneous equations. If we supply a guess of 6 inches for the length of the banana, the system responds by guessing that the weight of the banana is 12 ounces, but nothing else. There must be another simultaneous equation, so we must specify another variable to be relaxed. Due to the complexity of its constraint, we might guess that the age of the monkey or its mother needs to be relaxed. We can pick either one, and supply a guess of zero for its value. Now TK!Solver has enough information to solve this problem, and it tells us that the length of the banana is –1.75 inches! What did we do wrong?*

We got the wrong answer because we mixed units in our rules. We can fix the units problem by picking one set of units (feet and pounds, or inches and ounces) and putting everything into these units. Let us say we want to work in inches and ounces. We convert the rope linear density to inches per ounce, which sets its value to 0.44444444, and change the units for the length and weight of the rope. We must also change the second rule from rl = ma to rl/12 = ma since the problem gave this rule in terms of feet. After we do this, TK!Solver gives the length of the banana as 5.7499992, which is close enough to the correct answer (5.75 inches).

---

* This is the answer given by TK!Solver when the solution was typed in exactly from the book. It took some time to figure out where the error was.

This example points up a few limitations of TK!Solver. Unit conversions can only be applied to input and output variables, so if units are mixed in a problem the system will not figure out the correct conversions, nor will it flag an error. It is also inconvenient to have to specify which variables are to be relaxed, and to supply guesses for them. Despite its limitations, TK!Solver is a powerful problem-solving system, and it has enjoyed wide popularity.

4.1.4 Juno

"Juno is a system that harmoniously integrates a language for describing pictures with a what-you-see-is-what-you-get image editor" [Nelson 1984]. With Juno, a constraint-language program can be represented either in its textual form or by the image it produces. The user can edit either form, and the changes will be reflected back into the program.

The underlying Juno language is relatively simple. Juno variables represent points; a line is referred to by its two endpoints. There are four constraints on points:

HOR (p,q)	the line (p,q) is horizontal
VER (p,q)	the line (p,q) is vertical
(p,q) PARA (r,s)	the lines (p,q) and (r,s) are parallel
(p,q) CONG (r,s)	the lines (p,q) and (r,s) are of equal length

Since these constraints act on points, not lines, there can be a constraint on a line between two points without there actually being a line drawn between those two points. For example, the constraint VER (m,n) really only specifies that the points m and n have the same x coordinate.

Constraints are represented graphically as icons. For example, the HOR constraint is represented as a horizontally oriented T-square, and the CONG constraint as a drafting compass. If the user picks up the compass icon and selects four points, the corresponding CONG constraint is inserted in the program. The current drawing can be converted into a procedure, much like Sketchpad's macros, which can then be called like a primitive.

Juno uses a form of relaxation for constraint satisfaction. Since the PARA and CONG constraints are quadratic, local propagation would not be of much use, but a general relaxation method is not required either. Juno uses Newton–Raphson iteration to solve its constraints. Although faster than general relaxation, it still takes time proportional to the cube of the number of variables. Juno speeds up this calculation by having the user supply a guess for the initial value; this guess can be supplied either textually or graphically.

The main contributions of Juno are the way it represents constraints graphically and the ability to automatically construct a constraint program from a graphical representation. But Juno's intended domain is very limited. Its only data object is the point, and there are only four constraints on points. Drawing pictures with Juno is like doing geometry with a compass and straightedge. In addition, as discussed in Section 1.4, there is no way to specify *betweenness* so some figures are impossible to specify uniquely.

It would be desirable to adapt Juno's programming interface to a more general system so that new objects and constraints could be defined graphically without ever having to drop down into the underlying implementation language. A recent paper by Borning [1985b] provides a first cut at this by allowing the user to interactively edit a constraint graph to define a new constraint.

4.2 Constraint Languages That Use Symbolic Techniques

The remaining languages use algebraic simplification techniques to solve constraint programs containing cycles.

4.2.1 Steele's Constraint Language

The precursor to algebraic manipulation of constraint programs containing cycles was work done by Guy Steele and others, in the artificial intelligence lab at MIT. They implemented several constraint-satisfaction systems based on local propagation while investigating problem-solving techniques. While the language described by Steele [1980] does not actually use algebraic simplification techniques, their use is suggested. This language, however, is interesting for other reasons.

Steele's constraint language could be held accountable for its actions. As each constraint was satisfied, information was stored containing the rule that was used to satisfy the constraint, and what caused this rule to be activated. The user could ask the system why a certain answer was given for a problem, and the system could respond with a reasonable explanation, to various levels of detail.

The system also allowed values to be retracted, so that changes could be incrementally computed without re-solving the entire constraint program. This also allows the constraint system to make assumptions, and later retract them if they lead to invalid conclusions.

4.2.2 Magritte

Magritte is an interactive graphical layout system in the same mold as Sketchpad or ThingLab, written by James Gosling as part of his Ph.D. thesis at Carnegie–Mellon University [Gosling 1983]. It differs from the earlier systems mainly in that it does not use relaxation. Instead, algebraic techniques are used to transform graphs that cannot be solved using local propagation into equivalent graphs that can.

The only primitive objects understood by Magritte are scalar values, but Magritte, like ThingLab, has a type system that allows the user to define new data types. These objects are built up from scalars by putting them into structures. Unlike ThingLab, in Magritte the data objects are separate from the constraints that act on them. This difference is consistent with the philosophies of the languages used to implement these systems (ThingLab in Smalltalk, and Magritte in LISP). New constraints are built up from the primitive constraints sum, product, equals, and less than.

Gosling states that constraints should be "treated as full-fledged constrainable objects." He suggests treating a constraint as a Boolean predicate, and a constraint program as a conjunction of these predicates. This would allow higher-order constraints to be used, but unfortunately these ideas are not incorporated into Magritte.

The major contribution of Magritte is its use of graph transformations to break programs containing cycles. The graph transformer is automatically invoked from local propagation as needed. Gosling suggests that a good constraint-satisfaction system would have a number of techniques at its disposal. For example, local propagation could be used as much as possible, then transformation, and then perhaps relaxation or some other technique.

4.2.3 IDEAL

IDEAL is a language for typesetting graphics into documents. It was written by Chris Van Wyk as part of his Ph.D. thesis at Stanford (where it was called LELAND) [Van Wyk 1980], and is distributed as part of the Troff typesetting software from AT&T. This language has several features that set it apart from other constraint languages.

Constraints in IDEAL are expressed as equations, which are solved using the linear-equation–solving algorithm described in Section 2.1.7. This limits the constraints that can be solved to those that reduce to linear relationships, but in practice this is usually more than sufficient. For example, the simultaneous quadratic equations for finding the circle that passes through three points can be solved. The primitive objects in IDEAL are complex numbers, which are used both for numbers and points. Consequently, each constraint equation is really two constraints, one on the real parts, and one on the imaginary parts.

IDEAL allows images to be built up hierarchically, using **boxes**. For example, this is a definition for a rectangle:

```
rect {
     var ne, nw, sw, se, center, height, width;
     ne = se + (0, 1) * height;
     nw = sw + (0, 1) * height;
     ne = nw + width;
     center = (ne + sw) / 2;
     conn ne to nw to sw to se to ne;
     }
```

This box contains a declaration for seven local variables, four constraints, and a command to draw four lines.

The box `rect` defines a data type that we can use to create instances of rectangles, each specified differently if desired. When we call a box we can specify additional constraints, hopefully enough so that the system has sufficient information to draw it. For example, we can specify a rectangle by giving its center, width, and height.

```
call rect {
     center = (0, 0);
     width = 0.75;
     height = 0.5;
     }
```

Or we could give any other combination of information that uniquely constrains it, such as the position of two opposite corners, or the area and two adjacent points.

IDEAL also has a facility for repeating objects, called **pens**, mainly used for drawing dashed lines. This special-purpose feature was required only because IDEAL does not have any general-purpose control structures, such as iteration or recursion. There are also sophisticated graphics facilities for drawing curves and arcs, opaquing the interiors or exteriors of figures, and merging pictures.

Boxes in IDEAL allow new objects to be defined, but there is no corresponding facility to define new types of constraints. The only constraints are numeric relationships between complex numbers. This ends up making the language wordy. For example, in order to constrain two rectangles R1 and R2 to be equal, we cannot just say R1 = R2, we must supply sufficient constraints on their points to make them equal.

As an example of using IDEAL, let us draw four rectangles in a square with arrows going clockwise between them.

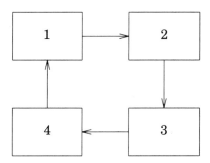

Figure 4.9   Output from IDEAL

If we assume we have primitives for rectangles and arrows (these are normally supplied in a library with IDEAL)* then the program to draw Figure 4.9 would look like this:

```
put r1: rect { center = 0; "1" at center };
put r2: rect { center = r1.center + (1.25, 0); "2" at center };
put r3: rect { center = r2.center + (0, -1); "3" at center };
put r4: rect { center = r3.center + (-1.25, 0); "4" at center };
put arrow { tail = r1.e; head = r2.w; };
put arrow { tail = r2.s; head = r3.n; };
put arrow { tail = r3.w; head = r4.e; };
put arrow { tail = r4.n; head = r1.s; };
```

IDEAL uses constraint satisfaction to allow the positions and sizes of objects to be stated as relationships, which makes it very easy to lay out complex figures. For example, we could place some rectangles side by side across the width of a page without specifying their individual widths, except that they are each to be of equal width. The width of each object will then be determined by the width of the page, even if the width of the page might change later, or even if the number of rectangles changes. This makes the description of images more flexible and natural.

The main drawback of IDEAL is its inability to define new types of constraints between objects. This severely limits its extensibility, and causes the descriptions of objects to be unnecessarily verbose.

---

* Note that the definition of rect in the library adds a few more variables, such as n, s, e, w, for the compass points at the center of each side.

4.3 Similar Systems

- Spread-sheet languages use some techniques similar to constraint satisfaction, but cannot be considered true constraint-satisfaction systems. As in the systems discussed above, the constraints in a spread-sheet are arithmetic relationships between numbers. When the user changes a number at the top of the sheet, the changes propagate down the sheet. This allows us to ask questions like "If I increase sales 7%, how much does my income increase?" Unfortunately, changes only propagate in a single direction (down), so statements in the language must be in order so that all values can be calculated in a single pass. In order to ask a question like "How much do I have to increase sales in order to increase income 5%?" we must try different values for sales until we get the desired result. This is the manual equivalent of relaxation.

- METAFONT, a system by Donald Knuth [1979] for describing typefaces, uses an equation solver that is similar to IDEAL's, except that it makes only a single pass though the equations before it gives up. Both Juno and IDEAL were in part inspired by METAFONT's ability to define equationally the lines and curves that make up a character outline.

- HEQS, a financial modeling language by Emanuel Derman, uses an extended version of the equation solver used in IDEAL [Derman 1984].

- EQLOG is a language that combines narrowing with term rewriting, resulting in a language that adds the power of a logic programming language to that of a constraint language [Goguen 1984]. Unfortunately, it has yet to be implemented, and other implementations of narrowing have severe execution-speed problems.

Chapter 5

Equation Solving

In the latter part of Chapter 3 we saw some simple examples of how to use Bertrand directly as a language. Bertrand's main purpose, however, is implementing other languages, in particular, constraint languages. In this chapter we use Bertrand to build a constraint-satisfaction system using the equation-solving algorithm discussed in Section 2.1.7. We will then extend it to handle Booleans and slightly nonlinear equations. We can use this new system directly to solve constraint problems, or we can use it as a base on which to build more-sophisticated constraint-satisfaction systems.

5.1 Solving Linear Equations

In order to implement an equation solver we need primitives for numeric constants and variables (bindable atoms). For numbers, we need the standard arithmetic primitives for addition, subtraction, multiplication, division, and so on. These may be implemented using floating-point, rational, or some other arithmetic. Numeric constants will be of the primitive type `'constant`.

For atoms, we need the primitive `is` operator to bind a value to an atom, but we also need other primitive operations. In order to construct ordered linear combinations we introduce a primitive to lexically compare two atoms called `lexcompare`. The infix `lexcompare` operator returns 0 if the two atoms are identical, -1 if the first precedes the second, or 1 if the second atom precedes the first. We will also need primitives to measure the "interestingness" of atoms; this concept will be explained in Section 5.2.

The heart of the equation-solving algorithm from Section 2.1.7 is the conversion of expressions into ordered linear combinations. Our ordered linear combinations will be given a type of `'linear`, which is a supertype of `'constant`. We also change the rule for the primitive `aNumber` operator so that

$$n: aNumber$$

creates an object named `n` of type `'linear` that represents the ordered linear combination $1 \times n + 0$. Ordered linear combinations are represented as a list of terms, with the constant term at the end of the list. If an object `n` is of type `'linear`, then `n.first` is the first term of `n`, and `n.rest` represents the remaining terms. These lists are constructed by the infix `build` operator. A term t consists of two parts: `t.variable`, the atom of the term, and `t.coefficient`, the variable's coefficient. Terms are constructed by the infix `buildterm` operator that takes a constant and an atom and returns a term.

We can now write recursive rules to add together or subtract two objects of type `'linear`. The prefix `merge` operator controls the order in which the terms are combined.

```
p'linear + q'linear { merge (
    p.first.variable lexcompare q.first.variable , p , q ) }
merge (0, p'linear, q'linear) {
    if (p.first.coefficient = -q.first.coefficient)
    then p.rest + q.rest
    else ((p.first.coefficient + q.first.coefficient)
        buildterm p.first.variable) build (p.rest + q.rest) }
merge (-1, p'linear, q'linear) { p.first build (p.rest + q) }
merge (1, p'linear, q'linear) { q.first build (p + q.rest) }
p'constant + q'linear { q.first build (p + q.rest) }
p'linear + q'constant { p.first build (p.rest + q) }
p'linear - q'linear { p + -1×q }
```

The case when p and q are both constants is handled by the primitive arithmetic operators. We will define the `if`, `then`, and `else` operators later, but their usage is standard. Likewise, we can define rules to multiply or divide a `'linear` by a `'constant`:

```
0 × p'linear { 0 }
k'constant × p'linear {
    ((k×p.first.coefficient) buildterm p.first.variable)
    build (k×p.rest) }
p'linear × k'constant { k × p }
p'linear / k'constant { p × 1/k }
```

Lastly, we can define rules to solve an equation.

```
p'linear = q'linear { 0 = p - q }
0 = p'linear ; d { p.first.variable is
    (p.rest / -p.first.coefficient) ; d }
```

Note the semicolon in both the head and body of the last rule, above. The equals operator can be used both to test for equality, or, with the semicolon operator, to assert equality. Since the `is` operator must only be introduced by an equation that is asserted to be true, this rule must only match an equation followed by a semicolon. Since the semicolon is an infix operator, it requires a right argument, the parameter variable d above. This dummy argument is merely passed through unchanged.

If a linear expression is asserted to be equal to zero, then it can be solved using the `is` operator. The last rule, above, does this by taking the variable in the first term of the linear expression and setting it equal to the remaining terms, divided by the negated coefficient of the first term. Note that if a linear term contains only a single variable, then the "remaining terms" contain only a constant.

The last rule above solves an equation for the atom in the lexically first term; but if we were using floating-point arithmetic and were worried about numerical accuracy, we could solve for the term whose coefficient is largest in magnitude. If we did this, then the rules above, combined with a few dozen rules for doing algebraic simplifications (see Appendix A), would completely implement the equation-solving system described in Section 2.1.7. As we shall see in the next section, however, this is not always what is desired.

It should be noted that although the above recursive rules for adding and multiplying objects of type `'linear` are correct, for efficiency they are not actually used in Bertrand. As with the simple numeric primitives such as numbers, linear expressions are treated as primitive objects, and addition and multiplication of linear objects are primitive operations. In addition, solving linear expressions that are asserted to be zero is a primitive, instead of using the `is` operator as in the last rule above. Making `solve` a primitive allows us to pick which variable is to be solved for based on how *interesting* each variable is.

5.2 Interesting Answers

If the answer to a set of equations is a constant, augmented term rewriting will always return that constant, regardless of which variables we solve for (see the discussion in Section B.5.3). If we always solved the equations to a constant (as in IDEAL), then there would be no reason to pick one variable to solve for over any other, beyond numerical-accuracy considerations. If the answer contains unbound atoms, however, we might get different answers, depending on which variables were solved for. For example, in the program

```
main { x = y + 2 ; y }
```

we are interested in the value of y, but there are two possible answers that can be returned. If the equation $x = y+2$ is solved for y, then the answer given will be $x - 2$, but if the equation is solved for x (which happens to be lexically first), then the answer given will be y. Of course, y is certainly equal to y, but this answer is not very interesting.

In the example above, y is the more "interesting" variable, since it is the atom we are asking the value of, so we would like to solve for it. Consequently, we introduce a partial ordering on bindable atoms that is a measure of how interesting they are. Initially, all atoms are of equally low interest. Atoms are deemed more interesting under the following conditions:

- Atoms occurring in the value of the *main* rule are the most interesting.

- Atoms occurring in the values of other rules are less interesting than those in the main rule.

- When an equation is solved for an atom (which must be the most interesting one), and its value contains other atoms, then they are set to be of the same interest as the atom solved for.

If there is no single most interesting atom in an equation to be solved, then from the set of most interesting atoms we must pick one. One way to do this is to pick the most interesting atom based on the lexical ordering of their names (this is easy to do since the linear expressions are kept lexically sorted). Note that we should *not* pick the most interesting atom based on some method that depends on the ordering of the statements in a program, since we would like the answer to a problem not to depend on the the order in which its statements are executed. For example, we should not pick the most interesting atom based on the order in which the variables were encounted by the interpreter (such as by hashing on the pointer value of their symbol table entries, as is often done by interpreters). By picking the most interesting atom based on their lexical ordering, the answer to a problem can change if the name of an atom is changed, but this can be used to advantage. For example, if we want to indicate that a certain variable should be solved for, we can give it a name with a lexically extreme value.

The above guidelines were developed experimentally, and they work reasonably well. More work should probably be done on understanding the semantics of interesting answers, and developing a better definition of an "interesting" atom.

5.3 Booleans

The rules in Section 5.1 were concerned only with solving simple equations. Other researchers have commented on the desirability of treating systems of equations as a conjunction of constraints [Gosling 1983]. A major advantage of using augmented term rewriting for solving constraints is that we can deal with arithmetic and Boolean constraints in a uniform manner. For example, the following rules define Boolean arithmetic:

```
false & a'boolean { false }
true & a'boolean { a }
~true { false }
~false { true }
~ ~a'boolean { a }
```

Note that because of the small number of constants in Boolean arithmetic there is no need for any machine-language primitives. Everything that is needed can be declared using rules. We can also define other Boolean operators in terms of the "not" (~) and "and" (&) operators defined above. For example,

```
a'boolean | b'boolean { ~( ~a & ~b ) }
a'boolean -> b'boolean { ~a | b }
```

The unary "not" (~) operator has the highest precedence of the Boolean operators, followed by the infix "and" (&) operator, then "or" (|), and finally "implies" (->).

The implication operator (->) can be used as an "if" statement, except that it is more powerful in that it can be used backwards. For example, if we assert

```
p = q -> r = s
```

then if we find that p is equal to q, we can assert that r is equal to s. In addition, if we find that r is not equal to s, we can assert that p is not equal to q.

It is also a fairly simple matter to define an if/then/else operator.

```
if a'boolean then b'boolean else c'boolean { a->b & ~a->c }
```

where if is a prefix operator, and both then and else are infix. Like the implication operator, this operator can be used backwards.

By adding rules for Boolean logic to the equation solver we can treat systems of equations as a conjunction of constraints, which allows us to express and solve higher order constraints. It also gives us conditionals, such as the if/then/else statement, which, along with recursion, makes Bertrand able to compute any computable function (Turing equivalent). Of course, standard term-rewriting systems are computationally complete, but augmented term rewriting allows Turing equivalence to be extended to equation solvers and other symbolic-algebra systems in a straightforward manner.

The above equation-solving rules can perform Boolean and numeric arithmetic, but so far we can only solve equations for numeric variables. An interesting exercise would be to develop additional rules to solve Boolean equations. Or we could abandon traditional real arithmetic entirely and develop rules for other arithmetics, such as for complex numbers, or even for the dimensions and tolerances used in mechanical design.

5.4 Reasoning with Equations

The above equation solver allows us to reason about objects without knowing their values. For example, the following simple problem defines two numbers and a relationship between them, and then asks a question about them:

```
main {
    m: aNumber;
    n: aNumber;
    m + 1 = n;
    m = n
    }
```

We want to know if m is equal to n. To show how the equation solver works, we will list the steps that might be used to solve this problem:

```
m: aNumber ; n: aNumber ; m + 1 = n ; m = n
true ; true ; m + 1 = n ; m = n
m + 1 = n ; m = n
1 × m + 1 = 1 × n + 0 ; m = n
0 = 1 × m + −1 × n + 1 ; m = n
m is 1 × n + −1 ; m = n      (the value n−1 is bound to m)
true ; 1 × n + −1 = n      (m was replaced by n−1)
1 × n + −1 = 1 × n + 0
0 = −1
false
```

This problem had a constant answer, but we could ask a slightly more interesting question:

```
main {
    m: aNumber;
    n: aNumber;
    m + 1 = 2 × n;
    m = n
    }
```

In this case, the answer is $0 = n - 1$, which means that the answer is true when n (or m) is equal to 1. The answer was stated in terms of n because the equation was solved for m. In this case, both variables were of equal interest, so the lexically first one was solved for.

The ability to reason about numbers is easily applied to other objects. For example, m and n could have been points whose positions are related by some complicated function, and we can ask under what conditions they coincide, perhaps to do collision detection. Or we can test geometric theorems. For example, if we bisect the sides of an arbitrary quadrilateral and connect the four midpoints, the resulting figure is a parallelogram. Existing constraint systems have "proved" this theorem by drawing the figure, and having the user observe that the resulting figure is a parallelogram. Since Bertrand can reason about objects without knowing their values, we can prove this theorem algebraically without making any assumptions about a specific quadrilateral.

5.5 Nonlinear Transformations

As discussed in Section 2.1.7, there are several nonlinear transformations that are useful for solving nonlinear simultaneous equations. Unfortunately, nonlinear transformations are not safe to make — they can result in incorrect answers. An advantage of using Bertrand is that we can make nonlinear transformations safe by adding constraints to check our assumptions. For example, the following rule performs cross multiplication:

```
a'constant = b / c { a × c = b }
```

If the value of c evaluated to zero, however, the denominator would vanish, rendering the solution invalid. We can check for this error by adding an additional constraint to the rule:

```
a'constant = b / c { c ~= 0 ; a × c = b }
```

If c eventually evaluates to zero, then the added constraint will evaluate to false, causing a contradiction (since the semicolon asserts it is true). An example equation solver, including rules for some nonlinear transformations, is given in Appendix A.

In addition to the rules above, there are many other possibilities. For example, we can define a set of rules to solve simple calculus problems. The following rules do simple differentiations:

```
diff a'constant  { 0 }
diff (x ^ n'constant) { n × x ^ (n-1) }
diff ( a + b )   { (diff a) + (diff b) }
diff ( a'constant × x)   { a × (diff x) }
diff ( f / g )   { (g × (diff f) - f × (diff g)) / g^2 }
```

We could also define rules for integration.

5.6 Word Problems

Let us now use the resulting equation solver to solve some constraint problems. For example, in Section 4.1.3, we used TK!Solver to solve a brain teaser about the length of a banana. In this section we use the Bertrand equation solver to solve the same problem. In the following program, an ellipsis (...) begins a comment that runs to the end of the line.

```
main {
    rld: aNumber;            ... rope linear density
    rl: aNumber;             ... length of rope
    rw: aNumber;             ... weight of rope
    bld: aNumber;            ... banana linear density
    bl: aNumber;             ... length of banana
    bw: aNumber;             ... weight of banana
    ww: aNumber;             ... weight of weight
    mw: aNumber;             ... weight of monkey
    ma: aNumber;             ... age of monkey
    Ma: aNumber;             ... age of monkey's Mother

    rld = 1/3 × 16 / 12;  ... oz / in
    bld = 2;
    ww = mw;
    rl / 12 = ma;            ... rope length in feet
    mw = Ma;
    ma + Ma = 30;
    mw / 2 + bw = (ww + rw) / 4;
    Ma = 1/2 × 3 × 1/2 × 4 × 2 × 1/3 × 3 × 1/4 × ma;
    bw = bl × bld;
    rw = rl × rld;
    bl
}
```

Bertrand's equation solver can handle these nonlinear simultaneous equations directly, instead of using relaxation as TK!Solver does. Not only does this relieve us of the need to supply guesses, it is also much faster, and the result is 5.75, not 5.7499992.

As with TK!Solver, while formulating the problem we had to be careful about units. We picked ounces and inches for the base units, and explicitly had to make sure all of the equations were stated in the correct terms. So when the problem said the rope's linear density was 1/3 pound per foot, we had to convert it into ounces per inch. In the fourth equation, we also had to divide by 12 to convert the rope's length back into feet.

The solution above uses Bertrand only as an equation solver, so it does not use the full power of the language. A better way to solve the above problem is to introduce a new data type called an object, which contains fields for `weight`, `length`, `age`, and `linear_density`. An instance of an object is created with the nullary `make_object` operator.

```
make_object {
    weight: aNumber;
    length: aNumber;
    age: aNumber;
    linear_density: aNumber;
    linear_density = weight / length }
```

Note that there is a constraint, the definition of `linear_density`, in the data type definition.

We can also introduce some rules to do unit conversions. The following "in_units" rules are all postfix operators.

```
x in_ounces { x }
x in_pounds { x / 16 }
x in_inches { x }
x in_feet { x / 12 }
x in_years { x }
```

Our problem specification is now almost identical to the original word problem (see Section 4.1.3).

```
main {
    rope: make_object;
    banana: make_object;
    monkey: make_object;
    mother: make_object;
    weight: make_object;

    rope.weight in_pounds / rope.length in_feet =  1/3;
    banana.weight in_ounces / banana.length in_inches = 2;
    weight.weight = monkey.weight;
    rope.length in_feet = monkey.age in_years;
    monkey.weight in_ounces = mother.age in_years;
    monkey.age in_years + mother.age in_years = 30;
    monkey.weight in_pounds / 2 + banana.weight in_pounds =
        (weight.weight in_pounds + rope.weight in_pounds) / 4;
    mother.age in_years =
        1/2 × 3 × 1/2 × 4 × 2 × 1/3 × 3 × 1/4 × monkey.age;
    banana.length
}
```

Because of the use of the postfix "in_units" rules, there is no need to be concerned about mixing units. All unit conversions are done automatically.

This example shows that Bertrand can be used simply as an equation solver, without defining new data types or operators (constraints), but that the ability to define new data types and operators makes it easier to solve problems.

5.7 Electrical Circuits

As a better example of how using rules to define data types can make solving problems easier, let us use the equation solver to build some electrical circuits, as was done using ThingLab in Section 4.1.2. We introduce a new data type, `'eob`, which stands for electrical object. Using rules, we define two types of `'eob` — a `resistor` and a `battery`.

```
resistance'linear resistor {
    voltagein: aNumber;
    voltageout: aNumber;
    current: aNumber;
    voltagein - voltageout = current × resistance
    } 'eob

voltage'linear battery {
    voltagein: aNumber;
    voltageout: aNumber;
    current: aNumber;
    -voltage = voltagein - voltageout
    } 'eob
```

The operators `resistor` and `battery` are both postfix, and take a single argument. The rule to define a resistor, which takes the resistance value as its argument, defines a resistor using Ohm's law. The rule to define a battery takes the voltage of the battery as its argument, and says that this voltage must be the difference between the input voltage and the output voltage. The voltage is negative because batteries generate voltage, rather than dropping it as in a resistor.

The following rule defines an operator for connecting electrical objects in series:

```
a'eob series b'eob {
    a.current = b.current &
    a.voltageout = b.voltagein
    }
```

This rule states that the current through two objects in series must be the same, and the voltage on the output terminal of the first must be equal to the voltage on the input terminal of the second.

As a measure of how easy it is to describe new objects and constraints in Bertrand, compare the above three rules with the equivalent problem definition written for ThingLab, in Section 4.1.2.* We can also define some rules to do unit conversions, and for "syntactic sugar."

```
n kilo { 1000 × n }
n volt { n }
n ohm { n }
ground { 0 }
```

Except for the nullary `ground` operator, these operators are unary postfix.

We can now solve the problem of hooking two 100-ohm resistors in series with a 10-volt battery.

```
main {
      b1: 10 volt battery;
      r1: 100 ohm resistor;
      r2: 100 ohm resistor;

      b1 series r1;
      r1 series r2;
      r2 series b1;
      b1.voltagein = ground;
      r1.current
      }
```

This constraint program is equivalent to the following schematic diagram:

---

* An earlier version of Bertrand did not require numbers to be declared, so the entire program to define resistors, batteries, and series circuits was three lines long.

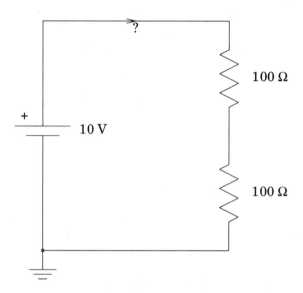

ThingLab used relaxation to solve this problem, but the Bertrand equation solver can solve these slightly nonlinear simultaneous equations directly. Our problem description is much more concise since, unlike ThingLab, we do not have to supply procedures for the local computation of each variable. Lastly, we can say that `r1` is an n `ohm resistor` and solve for the value of the resistor given a desired current. In ThingLab, the resistance had to be specified as a reference value so that the constraint satisfier would not try to change it.

Since we can solve this problem directly, there is no need to introduce a redundant view of two resistors in series. The advantage of this is that we can use the same rules to solve more-complicated problems. For example, we can solve for the resistance of a circuit with five resistors connected in a bridge (as shown in Figure 5.1), for which a human solver would have to use mesh analysis. An even more difficult problem is to connect 12 resistors as the edges of a cube, and ask for the resistance value across one of the major diagonals. This graph is not planar, so even mesh analysis cannot be used to solve it. As a measure of the difficulty of this problem, Bertrand's answer disagreed with the value computed by some human problem solvers. We finally built the circuit and measured it to confirm that Bertrand was giving the correct answer.

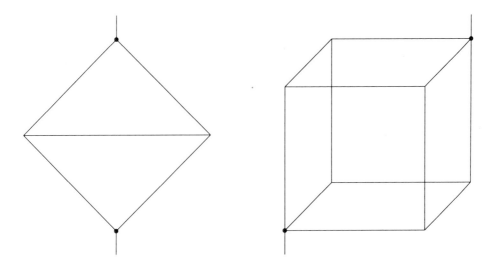

Figure 5.1   Resistance networks

Lastly, as mentioned in Section 1.3, we might want to add a constraint to make sure that we do not burn up a resistor by putting too much power through it. This would only require adding an additional variable and one additional constraint to the definition of a resistor:

```
resistance'linear resistor {
    voltagein: aNumber;
    voltageout: aNumber;
    current: aNumber;
    wattage: aNumber;
    (voltagein − voltageout) × current < wattage;
    voltagein − voltageout = current × resistance
    } 'eob
```

Chapter 6

Graphics Applications

6.1 Input and Output

Up to this point, all input to Bertrand has been performed by assigning values to variables, and all output was taken from the final value of the subject expression. This is acceptable for a system that is run in batch mode, such as IDEAL or TK!Solver, where all input is supplied before the program is run, and all output printed or displayed after the run is complete. Other constraint languages, such as ThingLab and Sketchpad, are run interactively, which contributes greatly to their utility. Interaction is especially important for graphics applications.

Simple interactive input and output (I/O), including graphic I/O, has been added to Bertrand by creating new primitive operators that, as a side effect, perform an input or output operation. For example, the primitive `read` operator is rewritten into a value read from the user's terminal. Since this value is used as an expression, the user can type in an arbitrary expression, not just a simple value. For example, a program could ask the user for the width of a rectangle, and the user could respond with an expression that constrains the rectangle to be one half as high as it is wide.

Likewise, the `write` operator takes a single argument, writes it out to the terminal, and rewrites to `true` if the operation was successful. The input and output primitives can optionally take a file name, and perform I/O to a file instead of the terminal.

Adding I/O primitives is relatively easy — the more difficult task is to synchronize input and output with the outside world. A major advantage of Bertrand is that its nonprocedural semantics allow operations to be performed in parallel whenever possible. When dealing with the outside world, however, this turns into somewhat of a liability. When one operation must precede another, an explicit dependency must be set up between them to make sure they are performed in the proper order.

For example, if we want to ask the user to enter the width of a rectangle using our `read` and `write` operators, we might write the following program fragment:

```
write "enter width of rectangle: "; rect.width = read;
```

Since statements are not required to execute sequentially, there is nothing to prevent the read operation from occurring before the write operation, causing the program to wait for input before it asks the question. To prevent this misordering, we must make the read operation depend explicitly on the write operation. For example, in the I/O library we could define the following rules:

```
ask s'string { (write s) then_read }
true then_read { read }
```

Ask is a prefix operator that calls the `write` operator with a string argument, and then calls the postfix `then_read` operator, passing to it the result of the write operation. The `then_read` operator waits until the `write` operation returns `true` before it is rewritten into a `read` operation. Our program fragment can now be changed to

```
rect.width = ask "enter width of rectangle: "; ...
```

and the correct sequence of operations is ensured.

For a long dialogue of input and output operations, explicit dependencies must be set up for each operation that is to be sequenced. This can be quite cumbersome, but fortunately there are other forms of interactive input and output that are easier to program using nonprocedural languages than the lengthy question-and-answer form that is most natural for conventional procedural languages. For example, the event-driven interaction used by the Smalltalk programming environment, and later by the Macintosh computer, is practically impossible to program using conventional single-thread-of-control languages without resorting to polling loops or interrupt handlers. In Bertrand, since there is no single thread of control, this sort of interaction would actually be easier to program than a conventional dialog. For example, in such an interface, multiple read requests could be made active at the same time; the user might select which request to respond to by pointing at it with the mouse, or possibly by selecting it from a menu.

6.2 Graphics

Existing constraint languages, such as Sketchpad and IDEAL, are particularly useful for describing graphical objects. Once the objects are described using constraints, these systems use traditional rendering techniques to draw them. Thus the abilities of constraint languages complement existing graphics research on rendering objects.

While the ability to output graphics is important for demonstrating that graphics constraint languages can be built using Bertrand, beyond demonstrating this capability, little work has been done to add all the graphics features that would be required to turn it into a full graphics system. Since Bertrand is an extensible language, once the graphics primitives are in place other features can be added using rules. In addition, the current implementation of Bertrand is run only in batch mode, so there has been no significant investigation into the problems of interactive graphic input and output (beyond adding the `read` and `write` operators, and operators to read graphic input from a mouse and write graphic output to a bit-mapped workstation display). Even so, Bertrand's graphic abilities compare favorably to popular (batch) graphics languages such as PIC [Kernighan 1982], mainly because of the *power* of being able to describe graphic objects using constraints and the *extensibility* provided by being able to define new data types and constraints.

Graphic output is currently done with a small number of primitive operators for drawing lines, circles, rectangles, and character strings at specified positions. We can also specify graphic input locations using a mouse. These primitive graphic operations have side effects, so the Bertrand interpreter had to be modified to add them, but the new data types and constraints (operators) can be added using standard rules. The first thing that is required for us to add is a data type for points:

```
aPoint { x: aNumber; y: aNumber; true } 'point
```

A point is created with the `aPoint` operator, and has two sub-objects, the x and y coordinates of the point. We can also define operations on points, for example,

```
p'point = q'point { p.x = q.x & p.y = q.y }
```

Two points are equal if their x and y coordinates are both equal. Note that the value of this rule is a Boolean, so it can be used both to ask if two points are equal, or to assert that two points are equal using the semicolon operator. Another operation on points is to sum two points:

```
p'point + q'point { r: aPoint;
    r.x = p.x + q.x; r.y = p.y + q.y; r }
```

The sum of two points is taken by summing the x and y coordinates and returning a new point. Other operations on points can be added in the same manner.

New data types can be built up hierarchically from the point data type. A line segment is defined by its two endpoints:

```
aLine { p: aPoint; q: aPoint; true } 'line
```

Again, we can define some operations on lines:

```
l'line = m'line { l.p = m.p & l.q = m.q }
l'line conn m'line { l.q = m.p }
horiz l'line { l.p.y = l.q.y }
vert l'line { l.p.x = l.q.x }
```

As well as a definition of equality, we have also added operators to connect two lines
end to end, and to constrain a line to be horizontal or vertical. The intuitive nature of
these rules is readily apparent. For example, the third rule defines a line to be horizontal if the y coordinates of its endpoints are equal. All of these operators can be
used either as assertions or as tests.

Again, building hierarchically, in Figure 6.1 we define a data type for an upright
rectangle:

```
aRect {
    left: aLine;      vert left;
    top: aLine;       horiz top;
    right: aLine;     vert right;
    bottom: aLine;  horiz bottom;
    left conn top; top conn right;
    right conn bottom; bottom conn left;
    true } 'rect
```

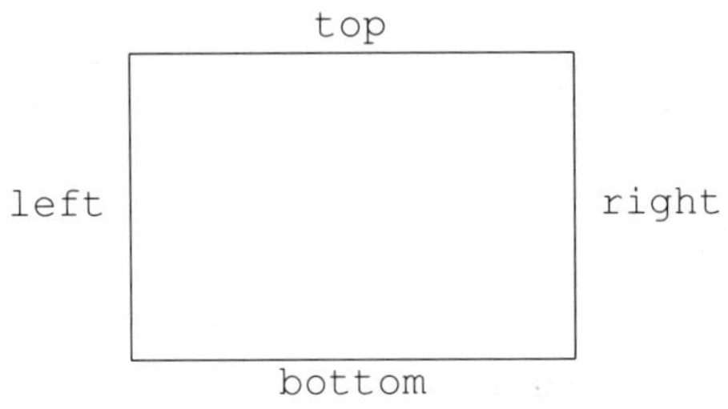

Figure 6.1   Data type for an upright rectangle

The data type for a rectangle has four sub-objects, but unlike the data types for line
and point, it also includes some constraints to connect the four sides together, and to
constrain the sides to be appropriately horizontal or vertical. Note that putting the
constraints on a part on the same line as its declaration is only a matter of style, both
the declarations and the constraints could occur anywhere and in any order inside
the body of the rule.

Redundant Parts

In the definition of a rectangle above, the corners of the rectangle can only be referenced indirectly. For example, the upper-left corner is either `top.p` or `left.q`. A
frequent and useful tactic is to add redundant parts to a data type, so that the user
can refer to these parts directly. We can add names for all the compass points of a
rectangle, plus its center, width, and height, by adding the following text to the
definition of a rectangle:

```
nw: aPoint;      nw = top.p;
ne: aPoint;      ne = right.p;
se: aPoint;      se = bottom.p;
sw: aPoint;      sw = left.p;
n: aPoint;       n.x = (nw.x + ne.x)/2; n.y = nw.y;
s: aPoint;       s.x = (nw.x + ne.x)/2; s.y = sw.y;
e: aPoint;       e.x = nw.y; e.y = (ne.y + se.y)/2;
w: aPoint;       w.x = nw.x; w.y = (nw.y + sw.y)/2;
c: aPoint;       c.x = n.x; c.y = w.y;
width: aNumber;     width = e.x - w.x;
height: aNumber;    height = n.y - s.y;
```

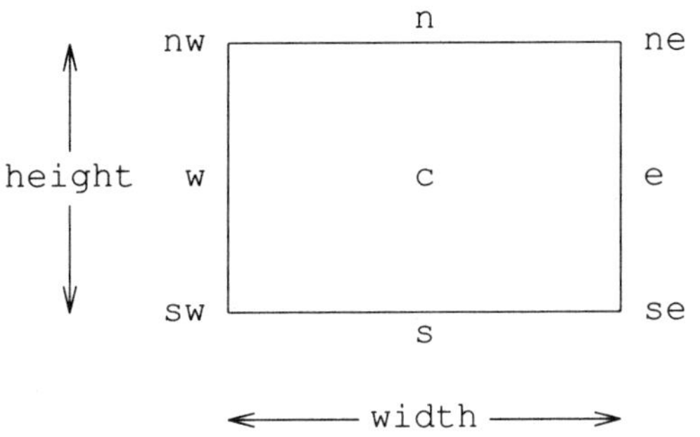

Figure 6.2   Adding redundant parts

As in the constraint language IDEAL, we can now define a rectangle in a multitude of ways. To draw graphic objects we introduce the postfix bang (!) operator, with the convention that a bang applied to any object outputs that object. For every graphic object we define a rule that matches that object followed by a bang, which rewrites to the appropriate primitive graphic operation(s). For objects such as lines, this operation is indeed a primitive. For composite objects such as rectangles, we define a rule such as

```
r'rect ! { r.left ! ; r.top ! ; r.right ! ; r.bottom ! ; true }
```

All of the rules above for defining graphic data types and operations can be put into a library, like the library in which the rules for solving equations were placed. The language user can then use these libraries to draw two-dimensional figures.

Since Bertrand is an extensible language, in order to draw three-dimensional objects we only need to redefine some of our graphic objects. For example, a point will need a z coordinate, and equality on points will have to check the z coordinate. But lines still consist of only two points, and rectangles consist of four lines, so their definitions remain intact. The availability of an additional dimension does open up new possibilities, however, such as a new data type for a rectangular prism made up of six rectangles.

6.2.1 Diagrams

To show how Bertrand can be used to build a simple constraint language for doing graphics, we will now define some rules for doing simple flow-chart type diagrams. Instead of using the data types for lines and rectangles from the previous section, we will define our data types from scratch to show how easy it is. All we will assume is the following primitive graphics operators (these operators, along with others including the operators from the previous section, are all provided in the current implementation of Bertrand).

```
(x, y, rad) ! drawcircle
(string, (x, y)) ! drawstring
(x1, y1, x2, y2) ! drawarrow
(left, top, right, bottom) ! drawrect
```

The `drawcircle` operator draws a circle with a specified position and radius, `drawstring` centers a string at the specified location, and `drawarrow` draws an arrow between two points. Upright rectangles are specified by giving the coordinates of the top-left and bottom-right corners (sometimes called "Manhattan style"). Since these operators are primitives, all of their arguments must become constants before they are invoked.

Besides the primitives above, the only other operator we need is

```
x inch { x × 100 }
```

The postfix `inch` operator converts numeric quantities in inches into device units for the current graphic-output device. In this case, our output device is a workstation with 100 pixels to the inch. Using this operator we can define all of our dimensions in device-independent units. If we change to a different device, we need only change a constant in this one rule.

Now let us define an object that is a box measuring 1.5 inches by 1 inch, with a string centered inside it:

```
box s'string {
     width: aNumber;      width = 1.5 inch;
     height: aNumber;     height = 1 inch;
     center.x: aNumber;   center.x = (left + right)/2;
     center.y: aNumber;   center.y = (top + bottom)/2;
     left: aNumber; right: aNumber; width = right − left;
     top: aNumber; bottom: aNumber; height = top − bottom;
     (left, top, right, bottom) ! drawrect;
     (s, center.x, center.y) ! drawstring
     } 'gob
```

Note that a variable name can be used in an expression before it is declared, if desired. Next, we define a rule for a circle with a string centered inside it:

```
circle s'string {
        width: aNumber;      width = 1 inch;
        height: aNumber;     height = 1 inch;
        center.x: aNumber;   center.x = (left + right)/2;
        center.y: aNumber;   center.y = (top + bottom)/2;
        left: aNumber; right: aNumber; width = right - left;
        top: aNumber; bottom: aNumber; height = top - bottom;
        (circle.x, circle.y, width/2) ! drawcircle;
        (s, center.x, center.y) ! drawstring
        } 'gob
```

This rule is the same as the rule for a box, except that a circle one inch in diameter is drawn. Circles and boxes are both of type 'gob, which stands for graphic object. Objects of type 'gob are arranged relative to each other with four infix operators called rightto, upto, leftto, and downto. Here is the rule for the rightto operator:

```
a'gob rightto b'gob {
    a.right + 0.8 inch = b.left;
    a.center.y = b.center.y;
    (a.right, a.center.y, b.left, b.center.y) ! drawarrow
    }
```

The other three operators are defined similarly.

Once these six rules are defined we can use them to draw diagrams. For example, the following constraint program draws a figure with four objects:

```
main {
    input: circle "constraints";
    process: box "bertrand";
    output: circle "pictures";
    program: circle "rules";

    input rightto process;
    process rightto output;
    program upto process;

    input.left = 0; input.top = 0; true
    }
```

The resulting diagram is shown in Figure 6.3:

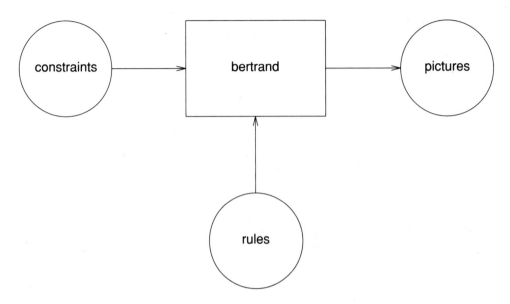

Figure 6.3   A diagram defined by constraints

Note that we did not have to supply locations for each object. Instead, the positions of the objects were specified relative to each other, and the system calculated their absolute positions. Of course, at least one object had to be given an absolute screen location. The last line of the constraint program gives an absolute screen location to the object named `input`. We can make this even easier by defining a rule:

```
origin a'gob { a.left = 0 & a.top = 0 }
```

The prefix `origin` operator places the upper-left corner of its argument at the origin of the screen, which (on our workstation) is the upper-left corner of the screen.

These six rules show how easy it is to define a simple constraint system for graphics. The same rules can be used to draw many different diagrams. For example, in Section 4.2.3 we used IDEAL to describe four rectangles connected by arrows. Compare IDEAL's description to the following constraints written in Bertrand:

```
r1: box "1";
r2: box "2";
r3: box "3";
r4: box "4";
r1 rightto r2;
r2 downto r3;
r3 leftto r4;
r4 upto r1;
origin r1;
```

Other examples of diagrams described using these rules are in Appendix A. Of course, with these few rules only simple diagrams can be described, but rules for more-complex diagrams are easily added.

6.2.2 Describing Graphic Objects

Computer graphics is often used to model real objects, as in applications such as Mechanical Computer Aided Design (ME-CAD). An advantage of Bertrand is that it allows a user to describe objects in terms more meaningful than just linear dimensions. The following example hints at how this could be used in a real application.

We wish to describe a metal plate with a number of screw holes; the holes are used to fasten the plate to something with screws. Instead of specifying the position of the holes, or even the number of holes required, we want to have them calculated automatically from other information, such as the force exerted on the plate. For example, we could specify such a plate with the following simple constraints:

```
force = 2.5 newtons;
length = 12 centimeters;
width = 1.2 inches;
```

We will discuss the rules to interpret these constraints later, but for now all we need to know is that our rules assume that each screw can hold 1 newton of force, so the above constraints define the following plate:

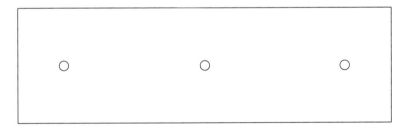

Figure 6.4   A plate that can hold 2.5 newtons of force

Instead of specifying the force, we could add a new constraint:

```
pressure = force / (length × width);
```

and then give the pressure on the plate instead of the force:

```
pressure = .25 psi;
length = 12 centimeters;
width = 1.2 inches;
```

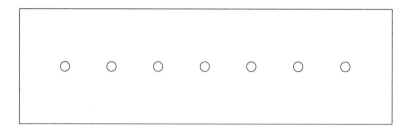

Figure 6.5   A plate that can hold .25 psi

The rules for solving equations can invert the (nonlinear) equation for pressure to calculate the force on the plate. If the pressure on the plate is changed, the number of holes will change.

```
pressure = .1 psi;
length = 12 centimeters;
width = 1.2 inches;
```

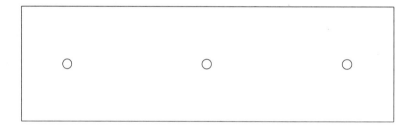

Figure 6.5   A plate that can hold .1 psi

If the length or width of the plate is changed, the number of holes should also change, since pressure is a function of both force and area. Before, when the force was specified instead of the pressure, the number of holes was independent of the size of the plate, and the spacing of the holes varied. Now, the spacing between the holes is (approximately) independent of the size of the plate (it varies only within the bounds required to allow the holes to be spaced evenly across the length of the plate), and it is the number of holes that varies, as shown in Figure 6.6.

```
pressure = .1 psi;
length = 5.5 inches;
width = 1.2 inches;
```

Figure 6.6   Another plate that can hold .1 psi

If the force had been specified, instead of the pressure, then the number of screw holes would have been independent of the size of the plate.

Note that in the constraints above we used several different postfix operators for units of measure such as `newtons`, `centimeters`, and `psi`. Like the postfix `inch` operator defined in the last section, these are defined using rules. In addition to converting standard measures into screen coordinates, we can use such rules to convert between units such as centimeters and inches, newtons and pounds, or psi and pascals. Of course, a set of these conversion rules can be placed in a library.

We have kept this example fairly trivial, but it is easy to imagine other examples. The thickness of a metal part could be dependent on how much stress it will be subject to, which might not be known until later in the design. The value of a constraint can be given as an expression, so that the proper value will be calculated later. For example, the size of a bolt holding on an aircraft engine may depend on the weight or thrust of the engine. The ability to delay the binding of design decisions allows the designer to work more abstractly, and thus gain expressiveness. Even if a value is later specified as a constant, the expression can be used to check that the value will be sufficient, and thus avoid a potentially dangerous design flaw.

We now discuss the rules and constraints that define the above plate with holes. The binding of the value of the number of screw holes was delayed by using an expression for its value. In fact, this expression is not a simple arithmetic expression; it includes a conditional:

```
if force>2 then numscrews = trunc(force)+1 else numscrews = 2;
```

This conditional expression ensures that there are at least two screw holes to hold the plate onto something. If the force is greater than 2, then it is truncated up to the nearest integer.

The following rule draws a circle to indicate the screw hole:

```
screw(x,y) { (x, y, .05 inch) ! drawcircle }
```

Note that `screw` could have been an infix operator, but we chose to simulate functional notation, with its two operands, the x and y position of the screw hole, separated by an infix comma operator. We can extend this rule so that it can take a list of numbers for the x positions of the screw holes by adding the following rule:

```
screw((head, tail), y) { screw(head, y); screw(tail, y) }
```

This rule places a hole at the head of the list, and calls itself recursively on the tail of the list.

Finally, we define some constraints to calculate the positions of the screw holes and place them in a list:

```
border = .5 inch;
spacing = (length - 2×border) / (numscrews - 1);
screw( numscrews from xpos + border spaced spacing, ypos);
```

The numbers `xpos` and `ypos` are the position of the center of the left side of the plate. The `border` is the distance to inset the screws from the edge of the plate. `Spacing` gives the distance between the screw holes. The last constraint above uses the operators `from` and `spaced` to generate the list of hole positions with the following rules:

```
n' constant from b spaced s { b, n - 1 from b + s spaced s }
2 from b spaced s { b, b + s }
```

The left-associative infix operators `from` and `spaced` are used to recursively generate a list of numbers, separated by commas. These rules generate a list of n numbers (the number of screw holes desired), starting with b (the position of the first hole), and incrementing by s (the spacing between the holes). In this case, we know from other rules that the number of screw holes must be an integer greater than or equal to 2, but we could have added explicit checks for this. The first rule applies when n is a constant greater than 2, and the second rule is the base case that applies when the number of holes desired is exactly 2. These rules act as an iterator; for example, the following input would be rewritten in the following way:

```
4 from 10 spaced 2
10, 3 from 12 spaced 2
10, 12, 2 from 14 spaced 2
10, 12, 14, 16
```

Also note that even though the positions of the screw holes are defined recursively, recursion has no procedural semantics. In fact, the current Bertrand interpreter does not draw the screw holes in order from left to right. Instead, a divide-and-conquer–like ordering is used (nine holes are drawn in the order 1, 3, 5, 7, 9, 2, 6, 4, 8). The actual order is not important; what is significant is that (as in the factorial example in Section 3.3.1) the lack of a procedural interpretation of recursion allowed the interpreter to reorder the execution. On graphics hardware with multiple processors (which is becoming common) the interpreter would have been free to use a divide-and-conquer scheme to split the process of drawing the screw holes over different processors, or to reorder the drawing of the holes to minimize the pen movement of a pen plotter, or sort them by scan line so they can be more easily rasterized for an electrostatic or laser plotter.

6.3 Streams

The example in the preceding section of a plate with holes and the factorial example in Section 3.3.1 both used recursion to define a **stream** of values that passed from a generator operator to a consumer operator, like data passed between coroutines. Since we already have the ability to generate and consume streams of data, we might consider using streams for input and output. The UNIX operating system uses a similar scheme. I/O streams can be set up between processes with a pipe, or can even be to or from a device. For example, input from and output to a terminal are treated as streams of characters, using the standard input, output, and error streams.

To use streams for I/O in Bertrand, we would have to change the `read` operator so that instead of rewriting to the value read from the terminal, it rewrites to a list whose head is the value read from the terminal, and whose tail is a recursive call to the `read` operator to read the next value. When the `read` operator encounters the end-of-file (EOF) indicator, it would return the empty list (or some equivalent end-of-stream indicator). We also change the `write` operator so that it can take a stream (list) of values, which it writes out recursively.

Our constraint programs using stream I/O are now filters. For example, the following program:

```
write (read + 2)
```

reads a stream of values, increments them by 2, and writes them out. In order for this program to work we must modify the definitions of operators such as + to take stream arguments. This modification is not quite as easy as it seems. If (as is the case above) one of the arguments to an operator is a stream, and the other is not, the nonstream argument must be converted into a stream. So, in the example above, the constant 2 actually represents a stream of constants, one for each value in the stream generated by the `read` operator (as in the language Lucid [Wadge 1985]).

Extending the semantics of operators so that they apply to streams as well as constants is easier if we do it on a case-by-case basis. In the plate-with-holes example, we extended the `screw` operator so that its first argument could be a stream with the rule

```
screw((head, tail), y) { screw(head, y); screw(tail, y) }
```

In the factorial example in Section 3.3.1, we added a similar rule to allow the product of a stream of numbers to be calculated. A more difficult problem is encountered with the `is` operator, which binds values to atoms. Since the values bound can be arbitrary expressions, we might imagine extending this operator to allow streams to be bound as the value of an atom. This requires that the value of an atom contain a recursive call to itself. Unfortunately, in Section 3.2.1 we made the restriction that the value of an atom cannot contain an instance of itself, in order to ensure single-assignment semantics for binding. This restriction makes streams second-class objects in Bertrand because they cannot be assigned as the value of an atom. Of course, this restriction could be relaxed in order to make streams first-class objects in Bertrand, but the semantics of the resulting language would have to be reworked.

Chapter 7

Execution

The current implementation of Bertrand is strictly an interpreter, but Bertrand has several important properties that make other more-efficient execution mechanisms possible. This chapter discusses several ways that Bertrand can be implemented, including interpretation and compilation on sequential machines, and finally by showing how the nonprocedural semantics of Bertrand would allow parallelism to be easily detected and taken advantage of by a multiprocessor.

7.1 Interpreting

The current Bertrand interpreter consists of three parts, a **pattern matcher** that repeatedly searches the subject expression for a redex, an **instantiator** that replaces a redex with the body of the rule that was matched, and a **name space** that manages the hierarchy of names, along with their types and values.

7.1.1 Pattern Matching

The pattern matcher takes a set of rules and converts it into a table-driven finite-state automaton. This automaton is constructed and interpreted using a pattern-matching algorithm that is similar to the one used in the Purdue Equational Interpreter [Hoffmann 1985]. This algorithm converts the problem of pattern matching on trees into the simpler problem of pattern matching on strings. The string pattern matching is then performed using a standard fast algorithm. The following description assumes some familiarity with the Aho–Corasick string-matching algorithm [Aho 1975].

The pattern expression in the head of each rule is a binary tree to be matched against a subexpression of the subject expression. Each pattern tree is flattened in preorder, ignoring the parameter variables, into an annotated string. Each element of the string is a triple that consists of the operator symbol at that node of the tree, and the tree movements required to get to the next element of the string. For example, the simple pattern expression:

```
true & A
```

which represents the tree

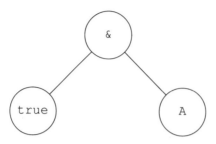

is flattened into the two-element match string:

    (& 0 left) (true 1 match)

The movement annotations consist of a nonnegative integer and an element from the set {left, right, match}. The integer gives the number of levels to move up the expression tree (toward the root) and the set element indicates whether to move down the left or right child to look for the next node to match. In the last element of the string, the set element is used to indicate that a match has been made, and the nonnegative integer indicates how far up the tree to move to get to the root of the matching expression.

    Let us see how this pattern would be matched against the subject expression

    true & x = 0

which represents the expression tree

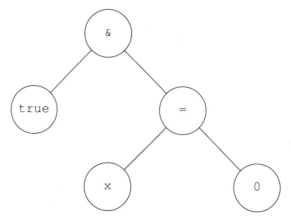

Starting at the root of the expression tree, the first element of the string says that the node we are pointing to must be the & operator. It is, so we move up zero levels in the expression tree, and then follow the left child. The next element of the string then says that the node we are pointing to must be the (nullary) `true` operator. It is, so we move up one level (to the `&` node) in the tree, and indicate that we have a match at that node. The right argument of the `&` operator was not examined because the pattern contained a variable in that position, which can match any expression.

A match string is generated for each rule in the program, and these strings are used to construct tables for an automaton using the Aho–Corasick algorithm. Each state of the automaton is annotated with the pair of movement instructions from the string. For example, consider the following pattern:

```
false & A
```

which corresponds to the match string

(`&` 0 left) (`false` 1 match)

We can combine this string with the string

(`&` 0 left) (`true` 1 match)

from above into the following automaton:

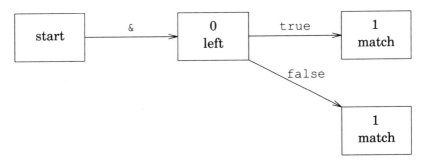

Strict Left-Sequentiality

Combining match strings in this way allows our automaton to run in time independent of the number of rules, since no backtracking is required for match strings that begin with the same prefix. Unfortunately, the automaton cannot be annotated consistently if different strings attempt to assign different annotations to the same state. For example, consider the pattern

```
A & false
```

which corresponds to the match string

(`&` 0 right) (`false` 1 match)

An automaton for this rule and either of the rules above cannot be annotated consistently because, after matching the & operator, the automaton does not know
whether to walk down the left or the right child. We say that these rules violate
strict left-sequentiality. Informally, strict left-sequentiality means that in a
depth-first, left-to-right traversal of a tree, we must always be able to determine
whether a redex has been found before we go on to the next node of the tree. Strict
left-sequentiality is defined formally by Hoffmann and O'Donnell [Hoffmann 1982].

Currently, rule sets that violate strict left-sequentiality cause an error at table-
generation time. Because of this restriction, parallel rules such as

```
true | A { true }
A | true { true }
false | false { false }
```

cannot be used, and must instead be written as

```
true | A { true }
false | A { A }
```

This can result in the left argument to "or" being evaluated unnecessarily when the
right argument is true.

This restriction, however, allows the resulting automaton to run very fast. It
can find a match in time proportional to the length of the subject expression, and
independently of the number of rules (certainly the lower bound for deterministic tree
matching). The time required to construct the tables for the automaton is also very
reasonable; it is linear in the total size of the match strings. The size of the resulting
tables is also linear in the same measure [Aho 1985]. Thus programs with hundreds
or even thousands of rules are practical.

Except for the parallel "or" case discussed above, rule sets that violate strict
left-sequentiality rarely occur in practice. In programming Bertrand only one other
violation has been encountered, and that was in the equation-solving rules. We could
overcome the left-sequentiality restriction by allowing the annotation at each state to
be a set of pairs, instead of just a single pair. The automaton could then try all the
pairs in the set until one succeeds. This scheme has the advantage that it keeps the
good performance characteristics of the Aho–Corasick algorithm for rule sets that are
strictly left-sequential, while allowing non–left-sequential sets with a reasonable
penalty. Because violations of left-sequentiality are so rare, this extension has not
been added to the current interpreter.

7.1.2 Instantiating Rules

Once the rule heads have been compiled into a table the pattern-matching automaton is started. When the head of a rule matches a redex in the subject expression the redex is replaced by a transformed copy of the body of the rule. This is called **instantiating a rule**. The body of the rule is transformed by replacing each parameter variable by a copy of its value,* and creating free instances of the local variables in the name space. In the example of matching in the last section, the only parameter was A, which matched the expression $x = 0$, so each occurrence of A in the body of the rule is replaced by the expression $x = 0$. Any remaining variables in the body of a rule are local variables. These local variables (none, in the above example) are inserted into the name-space tree.

The name space is stored as an *n*ary tree. The root of this tree is the top of the name space. When the `main` rule is instantiated, its local variables (the labels in the body of the rule) will be inserted into the tree as children of the root. As other rules are instantiated, their local variables are inserted into the name-space tree. For example, the rule

```
head { p: exp1 ; q: exp2 ; r: exp3 ; p + q = r }
```

contains three local variables (p, q, and r). If this rule matches the labeled redex

```
foo: head
```

then the three local variables are inserted into the tree as children of the label foo. Note that a label (such as foo) will always have been inserted into the name space before the expression it labels is reduced. For example, once the above rule is reduced, the labels p, q, and r will correspond to three new nodes in the name space tree. If exp1 then matches a rule with local variables, these local variables are inserted into the tree as the children of p.

The name of a name-space node is the label of the redex that created it. In the formal semantics in Appendix B, unlabeled redexes are automatically assigned a label with a generated name. Since in typical programs most redexes are unlabeled, the resulting name spaces would contain mostly generated names. Fortunately, it is not actually necessary to insert these names into the name space. Instead, the name space is stored as multiple, disjointed trees. An unlabeled redex starts a new root of the name space. This means that we do not have to generate names for unlabeled redexes, and also makes it possible to garbage-collect old names.

---

* If a parameter variable is only referenced once in the body of a rule then this copying is unnecessary. In the case of multiple references there are standard techniques for avoiding copying [-Mellish 1980], but they have not yet been used by a Bertrand interpreter.

Each node of the name-space tree also contains space for the value of the variable and its type. A variable has no value until one is bound to it by the `is` operator. A variable has a type if it was a label on a redex that matched a rule that was tagged with a type name.

Once the body of the rule that matched the redex has been copied, its parameter variables replaced by their values, and the local variables replaced by pointers to variables inserted into the name space, then it replaces the redex in the subject expression.

In addition to redexes found by pattern matching, another type of redex is an expression consisting of the `is` operator with a first argument that is a free variable (bindable atom). This type of redex is reduced by simply assigning the second argument of the `is` operator as the value of the first argument in the name space tree. A third type of redex is a variable that is no longer free because a value has been bound to it by the `is` operator. The bound variable is simply replaced in the expression tree by (a copy of) its value.

The process of finding a redex and replacing it repeats until no additional redexes can be found. At that point the subject expression is printed out and the interpreter terminates.

7.1.3 Types and Operators

In the pattern-matching algorithm presented above, parameter variables in the head of a rule were ignored when the match strings were constructed. If a parameter variable has a guard, however, it cannot be ignored, because it must match against a free variable of the proper type. Instead, we treat the type just as we would an operator. In an expression tree, each node has an operator, and the operator of a node representing a (free or guarded parameter) variable is the type of that variable. Consequently, the pattern

```
true & A'boolean
```

becomes the match string

(`&` **0** left) (`true` **1** right) (`'boolean` **1** match)

The third element of this string will match a node whose operator is the type name `'boolean`.

In the discussion above it is no coincidence that we are treating a type name as an operator. As mentioned during the discussion of supertypes in Section 3.2.3, type names and operators actually *are* the same thing. In fact, in the current implementation they are both stored in the same symbol table. Types can have supertypes, so all operators can have supertypes. A type name can always be distinguished from an operator name by the fact that it begins with a single quote, but even this is not really necessary (it does help with debugging, of course).

An operator that is not a type can be thought of as a functor that defines a mapping between selectors taken from the natural numbers from one through the arity of the operator, and the arguments of the operator. For example, a binary operator has two positionally distinguished arguments. Types are operators whose arguments are selected by name, rather than by position. For example, an object of type `'point` can have two arguments, its x and y coordinates.

In Prolog, unevaluated terms are used as data types. For example, a point can be represented as the term

```
point(X,Y)
```

Bertrand, like any term-rewriting system, can also represent data types this way. For example, we can represent a list using a comma as an infix operator:

```
head, tail
```

or we can represent it as a typed object, with two sub-objects named head and tail. Depending on which way we represent lists, a rule for a prefix operator that matches a single list parameter must be written in one of the following ways:

```
op (H, T) { expression involving H and T }
op L'list { expression involving L.head and L.tail }
```

The advantage of the second notation is that we do not need to know the structure of a data type to match it, nor does a human reader have to figure out what data type is being matched from its structure. Also, if we wished to take the head of the head of a list, the first rule's pattern would have to be changed to op((H,T1),T2), while the second rule's pattern would be unchanged. We would merely reference the variable L.head.head in the body of the rule. On the other hand, if we wish to match a list whose head is the constant zero, it is easy to change the first rule's pattern to op(0,T), while the other representation requires adding an additional rule.

Having two different ways to represent the same object can lead to confusion, especially since there are cases where either representation has advantages over the other. There should be a uniform representation for objects that allows us to refer to them using either notation, or possibly a single notation that has the advantages of both of the notations above. Some work has been done in this area [Leler 1984], but it was never included in a Bertrand interpreter.

7.2 Preprocessing Rules

There are a number of ways to improve the performance of the interpreter; most of these fall into the category of preprocessing. Currently, all rules (including rules in libraries) are read in and converted into tables for the pattern matching automaton every time a program is run. For programs of moderate size, the time spent constructing the tables is greater than the execution time of the automaton by an order of magnitude.* It should be possible to save the tables into some sort of "object file," so a program can be run repeatedly without "recompiling" it.

Even if the rules in the user's program are changed for each run, most of the table-generation time is typically spent processing the rules in the equation-solving and graphics libraries. Since these libraries rarely change, much time would be saved by preprocessing them, and for each run only linking their tables in with the user's rules.

The next step beyond linking rule tables together would be to allow rules to be dynamically added, deleted, or modified by the user. This would allow an interactive interpreter to be built so that the user could modify and run programs with only minimal delays for table generation. Adding new rules is quite easy — the current table-generation program can already do this, since it builds the tables a rule at a time. Modifying the bodies (right-hand sides) of rules is also easy, since it does not affect the tables, which are built solely from the heads (patterns) of rules. The hardest part is deleting rules from a table. If we could delete rules, modifying the head of a rule could then be done by deleting the rule and adding the modified one.

The last preprocessing trick we can use saves run time, rather than table-generation time. It is based on the observation that the right-hand sides of rules typically contain redexes that can be preprocessed out of the rule. For example, the meaning of a conditional expression is defined with the following rules:

```
if a then b else c { a -> b & ~a -> c }
p -> q { ~p | q }
f | g { ~(~f & ~g) }
~~d { d }
```

Each if/then/else expression in the subject expression will be matched by the first rule above. The body of this rule uses the implication operator twice, and the rule for the implication operator uses the "or" operator, which finally translates into an expression containing only the "not" and "and" operators. Since the rules of Boolean arithmetic are written in terms of the "not" and "and" operators, every if/then/else expression requires several rule rewritings before it is actually interpreted.

---

* For example, for the electrical circuits example in Section 5.7, on a 10 MHz 68010, table generation (for 82 rules) takes 3 seconds while run time (89 reductions) takes about .27 seconds.

This problem is compounded by the fact that Bertrand encourages rules to be built on top of existing rules. Luckily, we can easily get around this by preprocessing the right-hand sides of rules. For example, the first rule above could be preprocessed into the following rule:

```
if a then b else c { ~(a & ~b) & ~(~a & ~c) }
```

This rule rewrites an if/then/else expression into normal form in a single rewriting. Preprocessing rule bodies is especially effective for the equation-solving library, since the equation solver spends most of its time rewriting expressions into normal form.

One danger of preprocessing is that it violates the normal order rewriting of redexes that is required by our semantics to avoid infinite loops. For example, if the body of a rule to be preprocessed contains a redex that would match its own head, then the preprocessed body of the rule may be infinitely large. This case is not easily avoided, since it can also occur in an arbitrarily large set of mutually recursive rules. For example, a rule ρ_1 might contain a redex that matches the head of rule ρ_2, which contains a redex that matches the head of rule ρ_3, which contains a redex that matches the head of rule ρ_1. One fairly simple way to avoid this problem is to limit the depth (number of rewrites) to which preprocessing is done. This can result in a recursive loop being "unrolled" a few times (as in loop unrolling), so the depth of preprocessing can be used as a parameter to trade off between the space and time used for execution. Another solution is to keep track of each rule that is used in preprocessing, and simply not rewrite a redex if it matches a rule that has already been used.

7.3 Compilation

Programs in a constraint language define relations between objects. In order to compile these programs we must be able to convert these relations into functions. The resulting functions can either be directly interpreted or further compiled into machine code using standard techniques. Existing constraint languages have demonstrated that it is possible to compile constraint-language programs, and similar techniques can be used to compile Bertrand programs. Before examining how this would be done in Bertrand, let us recall how this is done in existing constraint-satisfaction systems such as ThingLab.

ThingLab uses propagation of degrees of freedom to find a path through a constraint graph from the outputs to the inputs, compiling "one-step deductions." In Section 2.1.4 this allowed us to compile a procedure for the temperature-conversion program once we knew which variable (F or C) would be supplied as input. It is important to note that even though we can generate code, there is no distinction between compile time and run time. A single program may be partially compiled and partially interpreted, or the system may pause to generate code in the middle of execution. Since compilation is done at run time, it should only be performed if the compiled code fragment will be used more than once, otherwise it is usually more efficient to use interpretation. This requires some mechanism to control when code is generated.

Some work has been reported recently on code generation using pattern matching and rewriting techniques [Aho 1985]. Since Bertrand is already based on pattern matching and term rewriting, this work can be naturally applied to allow Bertrand programs to generate compiled code. In some sense, one can write a Bertrand program to compile code for Bertrand programs. This is done by having the result of a rewriting be a code fragment that can be executed by some other rewriting. Consequently, compilation can be performed concurrently with other rewriting. How this is done is outlined in the following sections.

As mentioned above, compilation is worthwhile only if the compiled code can be used more than once. An advantage of Bertrand is that, since the generation of code is specified using rewrite rules, it can be controlled directly by the programmer, using existing mechanisms. In the following discussion, however, we will avoid these issues and assume that compilation is being performed at preprocessing time. Since preprocessing is also done using term rewriting, the same techniques are applicable at run time.

7.3.1 Compiling Simple Arithmetic Constraints

An augmented term-rewriting system can intermix compilation with interpretation by combining rules that generate code with other rules. To understand how compilation would work for arithmetic constraints, let us look at how arithmetic is done in the current interpreter. The equation-solving library contains rules for doing arithmetic such as

```
A'constant + B'constant { primitive to return sum of A and B }
```

As discussed in Section 3.1.1 this rule represents a large set of rules of the form:

```
1 + 0 { 1 }
1 + 1 { 2 }
1 + 2 { 3 }
 . . .
```

Arithmetic is performed when both of the arguments to an arithmetic operator become constants.

Compilation is based on the idea that, instead of waiting for a variable to become a constant and then doing arithmetic, if we know which variables will become constants, then we can generate code to perform the arithmetic when they do become constants. This has the same effect as the "mode declarations" sometimes used in compiling Prolog programs, except that the required mode information is inferred automatically (using the rule-typing facilities of Bertrand), instead of requiring the user to explicitly supply such information. This is similar to the way propagation of degrees of freedom works.

Propagation of degrees of freedom detects which variables will become constants by looking for variables with only one constraint (the outputs) and working backwards to the inputs. Instead, if we know which variables are inputs, then we can "propagate" knowledge of which variables will become known when the input is supplied (we assume the input is supplied as a constant value, not an expression). For example, our system might contain a built-in variable called mousey that returns the y coordinate of the mouse when a mouse button is depressed. We give this variable a type of `'input` to indicate that it will rewrite to a constant value as the result of an input operation. We can now add some rules to our equation-solving library:

```
A'input + B'constant  { generate code to add A to B }
```

This rule rewrites into a code fragment to add the input value A to the constant B. Since the variable mousey is of type `'input`, the expression

```
mousey + 32
```

will rewrite into a fragment that adds 32 to the y value of the mouse. Since the value returned by this fragment will also become a constant, we would like to continue compiling code if possible. Unfortunately, the rule above generates code only for variables of type `'input`.

To start generalizing the above rule, first we introduce a new type called `'lambda`. An object of type `'lambda` represents an expression (written as a function) that takes a constant argument and evaluates to a constant. (The argument and result can be structured objects, of course.) The operators in a lambda expression have their traditional mathematical meanings. We also introduce a primitive prefix apply operator that takes a lambda expression and a constant and evaluates the function represented by the lambda expression applied to the constant.

Our rules for arithmetic are then augmented with rules of the form

```
I'input + 1  { apply ("λx.x + 1", I) }
```

where the lambda expression (in quotes) is a function that adds 1 to its argument (the input variable I) when I becomes a constant. Note that the plus sign inside the lambda expression is the mathematical addition operator, not the Bertrand plus operator.

Rather than have a separate rule for each constant, we will parameterize our lambda expressions:

```
I'input + C'constant { apply ("λx.x + [C]", I) }
```

The variable C in brackets inside the lambda expression indicates that it is a regular (constraint) expression, not a lambda expression, and is subject to substitution by the term-rewriting system. This rule rewrites

```
mousey + 32
```

into

```
apply("λx.x + 32", mousey)
```

We would like to continue compiling constraints into functions, but unfortunately the above rule still works only on objects of type 'input. Rather than define new rules, we simply define a new type called 'known that is a supertype of both the apply operator and the type 'input. The above rule can then be slightly changed into

```
I'known + C'constant { apply("λx.x + [C]", I) }
```

This rule compiles code only for the + operator, but we can add similar rules for other operators, such as

```
I'known × C'constant { apply("λx.x × [C]", I) }
```

If we apply these rules to the expression

```
mousey × 1.8 + 32
```

it will be rewritten into

```
apply("λx.x + 32", apply("λx.x × 1.8", mousey))
```

Finally, we can write a rule to combine two nested apply operators:

```
apply(L1'lambda, apply(L2'lambda, C)) {
    apply(merge(L1,L2), C) }
```

where the merge operator performs the functional composition of two lambda expressions. This can be done using standard term rewriting (see Section 7.3.2). For example, the expression above becomes

```
apply("λx.x × 1.8 + 32", mousey)
```

The resulting objects represent the application of simple arithmetic functions to constants. To execute apply terms, we define the following rule:

```
apply(L'lambda, C'constant) { evaluate L with argument C }
```

This rule will wait until C becomes a constant (for example, when mousey becomes a constant because a mouse button was depressed) before evaluating the lambda expression.

7.3.2 Why Lambda?

In the rules and expressions above we enclosed expressions of type `'lambda` in double quotes so that they would not be confused with regular (constraint) expressions. Actually, the only differences between lambda expressions and other expressions are the operators. The operators in a lambda expression represent functions (noninvertible procedures) that take an argument and return a value. Operators in a constraint expression represent relations.

If we rename all of the operators used in lambda expressions with names that are distinct from their constraint-language cousins, then we can freely mix the two types of operators in expressions. We make the type `'lambda` a supertype of these new, distinct operators. Consequently, the term-rewriting system can be used to transform expressions containing lambda operators or the regular operators, or both. The user's manual for the Purdue Equational Interpreter gives examples of using rewrite rules on lambda expressions [O'Donnell 1985].

For example, let the functional versions of the operators + and × be ⊕ and ⊗, respectively. These new operators are subtypes of type `'lambda`. For notational consistency with other operators in Bertrand, we will also change the λ operator to be infix, so that λx.e will now be written x λ e. The rules to perform compilation become

```
I'known + C'constant { apply(x λ (x ⊕ C)), I) }
I'known × C'constant { apply(x λ (x ⊗ C)), I) }
```

The variable x in these rules is now a regular Bertrand local variable, so it will automatically be prefixed with a (possibly generated) label name when either of these rules is instantiated. This will keep different instances of x from interfering with each other.

The expression

```
mousey×1.8 + 32
```

will now be rewritten into

```
apply(x λ (x⊗1.8 ⊕ 32), mousey)
```

We used lambda calculus notation in the examples above mainly because of its familiarity. We just as easily could have compiled into some other form, such as combinator expressions [Curry 1958], data-flow graphs [Ackerman 1982], or even into a machine language. For example, let us compile the expression in the example above into assembly code. For simplicity we will assume a standard single address machine with an accumulator, but most any architecture (including multiple–general-purpose-register and stack architectures) would work as well. The instruction set for this machine includes

```
LOAD X        ... load the accumulator with X
ADD X         ... add X to the accumulator
MUL X         ... multiply by X to the accumulator
```

The operand X can be either a constant or the address of a variable. We will treat each of these instructions as a prefix operator, all of which are subtypes of a type `'code`. The rules for compiling code now become

```
I'known + C'constant { apply(ADD C, I) }
I'known × C'constant { apply(MUL C, I) }
```

We perform the composition of two pieces of machine code by simply concatenating them, so that one will execute before the other. Following the syntax of most assembly languages, we will indicate that two machine instructions are to be executed in sequence by placing a new line character (⏎) between them. Since Bertrand likes to treat everything as an operator, we will represent the new line character explicitly as an infix operator:

```
apply(M1'code, apply(M2'code, C)) {
    apply((M2 ⏎ M1), C)  }
```

Such a sequence of machine instructions is also made a subtype of type `'code` (by simply making the new line operator be a subtype of type `'code`). The rule to evaluate `apply` terms becomes

```
apply(M'code, C'constant) {
    execute LOAD C ⏎
            M  ;
    return accumulator as the result of this rule
    }
```

Consequently, our familiar expression

```
mousey × 1.8 + 32
```

is rewritten into

```
apply(MUL 1.8 ⏎ ADD 32, mousey)
```

When mousey becomes a constant, the instruction stream

```
LOAD mousey
MUL 1.8
ADD 32
```

is executed, and the contents of the accumulator is returned as the value of the `apply` expression.

7.3.3 Compiling Higher-Order Constraints

Bertrand treats a system of constraints as a conjunction of Boolean expressions. This allows us to treat conditional expressions and other higher-order constraints in a uniform manner. The compilation techniques for arithmetic expressions can be extended to higher-order constraints by adding rules for Boolean expressions. Note that in this section we return to using the notation of lambda calculus for our compiled expressions.

A typical higher-order constraint, the expression

```
p ~= 0  ->  q = 5  ;
```

asserts that if p is not equal to zero, then q is equal to five. In a constraint language the implication operator (like all operators) represents a relation, so this expression also means that if q is not equal to 5, then p must be equal to zero. Consequently, we cannot compile this expression until it is known which variable will be the input.

The equation-solving library contains rules to rewrite Boolean expressions into a normal form containing only the & and ~ operators (see Section 5.3). These rules rewrite the expression above into

```
~ (  ~ (p = 0)  &  ~ (q = 5))  ;
```

This is as far as we can take this expression until either p or q becomes a variable of type 'known. If p becomes known then, using the techniques discussed in Section 7.3.1, we can rewrite the expression ~ (p = 0) into an object of type 'known. Likewise, if q becomes known, then ~ (q = 5) will become known.

The expression above is of the form of a NAND expression:

```
~ (F & G)
```

where F and G are expressions that might become known if p or q become known. This expression can be read as saying that F and G cannot both be true for the expression to be true. If p were to become known (causing F to become known) we could use the rule

```
~ (F'known & G)  { apply("λx.if x then [~G] else true", F) }
```

to compile a conditional lambda expression.* This rule says that if F is true, then G must be false, but if F is false, then the expression ~ (F & G) is true, regardless of the value of G. Note that in this rule the lambda expression contains the expression ~ G in square brackets, indicating that the "not" operator is a normal Bertrand operator.

---

* The lambda expression if A then B else C is equivalent to the LISP (if A B C).

If p becomes known, then the expression above can be rewritten to

```
apply("λx.if x then [~~(q=5)] else true",
    apply("λx.not(x=0)", p)) ;
```

The two lambda expressions can be combined, resulting in

```
apply("λx.if not(x=0) then [~~(q=5)] else true", p) ;
```

Finally, the two consecutive not operators can be eliminated by the term-rewriting system, resulting in the expression

```
apply("λx.if not(x=0) then [q=5] else true", p) ;
```

On the other hand, if q were to become of type 'known, instead of p, causing G to become known, we could use a rule

```
a & b'known { b & a }
```

to reduce this case to the same situation as above. The resulting expression would be

```
apply("λx.if not(x=5) then [p=0] else true", q) ;
```

When q finally does become a constant, if it is not equal to 5 then the expression above rewrites to

```
p=0 ;
```

which will cause the value zero to be bound to p (by the interpreter). If q is equal to 5, then it rewrites to:

```
true ;
```

because nothing can be deduced about the value of p if q is 5.

In the example above we did not compile the binding operation, but we could have if we had a procedural (lambda expression) version of the is operator. To make sure that the is operator is used only if equality is asserted, we include the semicolon operator explicitly in the rule that does the compilation. The rule where F became known becomes

```
~(F'known & G) ; { apply("λx.if x then [~G ;]
        else [true]", F) }
```

The resulting of applying this rule to the original expression with F known would be

```
apply("λx.if not(x=0) then [q=5 ;] else [true]", p)
```

the constraint expression q = 5; could then be rewritten to q ← 5, and the resulting expression would be

```
apply ( "λx.if not(x = 0) then q ← 5 else [true]", p)
```

The left-arrow operator (←) used in lambda expressions is semantically very similar to the `is` operator. It binds a value (which must have been a constant) to a variable, and rewrites to (returns the value) `true`.

If, as in the example above, more than one variable could become known, we can use a greedier approach to compilation. We treat the question of which variable will become known as a conditional expression. For example, we could create the lambda expression

```
"λx.if known(x) then [exp]"
```

and then compile `exp` as if the argument of the lambda expression were actually known. In the example above, we could use this technique to compile code for the conditional expression for both the case where `p` becomes known, and where `q` becomes known. When either `p` or `q` actually does become known (becomes a constant) then we can use the appropriate code fragment without pausing to compile it.

We could use this technique on the temperature-conversion program to compile code to convert `F` into `C` and `C` into `F`, and allow the user to supply values for either one. We must use this technique sparingly, however, since it can result in quantities of code being generated for cases that might never occur. Worse, a program with many conditionals might generate code for each possible combination of inputs, leading to an explosion of generated code. Code should be generated only for cases that we expect our program to encounter frequently. Since in general there is no way for the compiler to deduce this information, compilation should be under the control of the user. In Bertrand, the user controls compilation by specifying which variables will become, or might become, known.

A Bertrand program will then become a combination of compiled code that can be executed by the machine, and some remaining constraint expressions that continue to be interpreted. Interpreted expressions can result both from expressions containing variables not of type `'known`, and from constraint expressions, possibly containing known variables, that are too complex to be converted into lambda expressions. For example, a set of simultaneous nonlinear equations might become linear (and compilable) depending on the value of one of the variables. We *could* test for such conditions in a lambda expression, but it probably is not worth the trouble of compiling for each special case.

7.3.4 Code Generation and Optimization

As shown above, it is possible to use term rewriting itself to generate machine code for Bertrand programs. One advantage of this is that if the machine code is generated by a set of rewrite rules, then different sets of rules can be used to generate code for different machines. Alternatively, in graphics it is common to use systems that include one or more separate graphics processors in addition to the host processor. A Bertrand program could be written that partitions the generated code between heterogeneous processors according to their capabilities.

In addition, some code-optimization problems, such as optimal assignment of registers, memory locations, and other resources, can be treated as constraint-satisfaction problems. This would allow further optimizations to be made on code generated by rules. For example, the Mumble microcode compiler for the Cm* multiprocessor used constraint-satisfaction techniques to assign microinstructions to microwords optimally [Gosling 1980].

As mentioned above, compilation is worthwhile only if we are going to use the compiled code many times, otherwise we should just go ahead and use interpretation. If we perform compilation at preprocessing time, for example, on the rules in the equation-solving library, then it is a safe assumption that these compiled rules will be used many times. If compilation is performed at run time, however, we can still control the generation of code by designating variables to be of type `'known` (or `'input`), otherwise the interpreter is used. Since the Bertrand interpreter does not treat compiled code differently from any other expression, such code can match a parameter variable in the head of a rule, or can even be bound to a free variable (bindable atom). This makes it easy to create and use multiple copies of compiled code.

Input requests, such as the reference to the variable `mousey` above, will often occur inside of a recursive rule that repeatedly reads an input value and performs some action. Using the techniques discussed above, these recursive rules can be precompiled, and the resulting code used repeatedly on a stream of input values. Note, however, that if our preprocessor avoids infinite loops by not preprocessing recursive calls, then each invocation of even a compiled recursive rule will require at least one rule rewriting by the interpreter. If instead the recursive rule is unrolled during preprocessing, then some of these rewritings are avoided, but, like any loop unrolling scheme, at the possible cost of some extra computation when the recursion terminates.

By using a combination of compilation and interpretation, very effective code can be generated. For example, the expression

```
s + 2 = 2 × s;  -8 + mousey + (s × 4)
```

will be rewritten using existing simplification rules in the equation-solving library into the much simpler expression

```
mousey
```

rather than generating code to perform the unnecessary arithmetic. This is similar to constant propagation techniques used by optimizing compilers, but since compilation is done concurrently with rewriting, there are typically many more constants available to propagate. In graphics, for example, a commonly used routine is one to multiply a stream of points by a 4-by-4 matrix representing a graphic transformation. If the matrix, whose elements will become known only at run time, represents a translation (one of the most common graphic transformations), it will contain many ones and zeros that can be propagated out. This turns a matrix multiplication (64 scalar multiplications and 48 scalar additions) into just three scalar additions, which can then be compiled. The resulting compiled code can then be applied to a sequence of points describing some object to be drawn.

7.4 Execution on Parallel Processors

An important unsolved problem is how to execute programs on parallel processors. The availability of cheap microprocessors that can be hooked together to form large but inexpensive computing engines has made finding an answer to this problem imperative. Unfortunately, just because we can hook hundreds or even millions of processors together does not mean that we can run programs any faster.

My original interest in constraint languages started while working on ways to execute graphics programs faster. The abundant parallelism available in most graphics algorithms led to an investigation of parallel data-flow architectures, including a machine design that (in simulation) executed graphics programs very rapidly [Leler 1983]. Unfortunately there was no easy way to program this processor, a problem that seems to be common among parallel processors. So while there was parallelism in the algorithms and in the processor, there was still no easy way to connect the two to take advantage of it. The problem was that it is much harder to write parallel programs than sequential programs, and sequential programs are hard enough to write to begin with.

On the other hand, constraint languages have been proposed as a way to make graphics programming easier, but since constraint languages are also nonprocedural they are amenable for execution on highly parallel processors. So, at least for some applications, constraint languages may make it much *easier* to write parallel programs. Some researchers had noted the similarity between constraint graphs and data-flow graphs [Steele 1980], but no further work has been done in this area.

A major problem in translating traditional languages to execute on parallel processors is that their procedural semantics prescribe a specific order of program execution. Since the semantics of these languages depends on statements being executed in the proper order, a compiler changes this order only with great effort.

If a set of rules for a term-rewriting system is *confluent*, then the order in which the rules are applied to the subject expression does not affect the result. This allows rewritings to be done in any order, even in parallel. We used this property to set up automatic pipelining for a factorial program in Section 3.3.1, and for a graphics program in Section 6.2.2.

When term rewriting is augmented by allowing binding of values to atoms, then the system is still confluent regardless of the order of the bindings modulo equality over expressions (see Section B.5.3). Unfortunately, if binding is allowed to be done in parallel, we run the danger of violating single-assignment semantics. For example, if the expression

$$\ldots \; ; \; x \; = \; p-1 \; ; \; \ldots \; ; \; x \; = \; q+1 \; ; \; \ldots$$

is split across two processors so that the equation on the left is being rewritten on processor A, and the equation on the right is being rewritten on processor B, then processor A might try to bind $p-1$ to x, while at the same time processor B is trying to bind $q+1$ to x. This would not be a problem on a single processor since, once a value is bound to x, all other instances of x are replaced by its value, preventing another value from being bound to it.

One way to avoid this problem on a multiprocessor is to keep the name space on a single processor, but this reduces parallelism and requires communication every time a variable is encountered to check if a value has been bound to it by another processor. Before a value could be bound to a variable, it would have to be locked, so that no other processor will try to bind a value to it.

A better solution is to simply keep separate name spaces on separate processors and allow different values to be bound to the same variable in different name spaces. At some point both processors will have rewritten their subject expressions as far as they can and will need to combine their answers. This is done by concatenating their subject expressions and doing a merge on their separate name spaces. If the same variable has a value in both name spaces, then one of the values is discarded, and a constraint is added to the subject expression that equates the two values.

In the example above, if processor A thinks the value of x is $p-1$, and processor B thinks the value of x is $q+1$, then when the name spaces are merged one of these values, say the value on processor B, is discarded, so the value of x in the merged name space is $p-1$. It does not matter which value of x is kept (except that we might choose which value to keep based on which variable is more "interesting"). In addition, the constraint $p-1 \; = \; q+1$ is added to the merged subject expression. Since $p-1$ and $q+1$ are both equal to x, they are certainly equal to each other, so the added constraint is valid.

In the expression returned by processor A, all occurrences of x were replaced by $p - 1$; on processor B, all occurrences of x were replaced by $q + 1$. The purpose of the added constraint is to allow the expressions in terms of p and q to be unified. If the equation $p - 1 = q + 1$ is solved for p, then all expressions containing p will be rewritten into equivalent expressions in terms of q. This will restore confluence, modulo equality over expressions.

The added constraints should not have a significant impact on performance because they can only be created as a consequence of a name being bound twice. Unlike Prolog, where one or more bindings will occur for each rule invocation, in Bertrand binding occurs relatively infrequently. Binding the same name twice should be an even rarer occurrence.

Augmented term rewriting allows quite a bit of flexibility in writing an interpreter for a multiprocessor. For example, as discussed above, each processor could contain all the rules, and the subject expression could be dynamically split among the processors. When a subject expression in a processor exceeds a certain size, it can send subexpressions to other processors, along with a copy of the name space. We can use virtual copies of the name space and only fetch entries on demand to avoid excessive copying. When a child processor finishes rewriting its subexpression, it sends the resulting expression and name space back to its parent to be merged.

Another approach partitions the rules onto different processors. This partitioning is done so that the rules on one processor interact minimally with the rules on other processors. For example, in Section 7.3 we defined rules to convert regular Bertrand (constraint) expressions into expressions containing procedural operators (lambda expressions). These rules could reside on one processor. A separate processor could be set up with the rules for compiling the lambda operators into machine code. Yet a third processor could do the actual execution of the machine-language programs. This sets up a pipeline, where all execution is done on one processor, compilation on another processor, and interpretation of the user's rules on another processor, all concurrently.

If, as discussed in Section 7.3.4, we are compiling and executing fragments of machine code interleaved with interpreted code, the compiled code fragments can be split between different processors. As mentioned above, these processors do not need to be homogeneous. One could be a graphics processor, another could be a floating point unit, and another could perform I/O operations. The interpreter, which could itself be split between different processors, could do remote procedure calls on the code fragments residing on the different processors. If the network architecture does not have uniform access cost for all processors (such as a hypercube network), then smaller compiled fragments could be assigned to nearby processors, while large fragments could be sent to distant processors.

7.4.1 Data Flow

In Section 7.3 we compiled constraint programs into procedural expressions. Because of the nonprocedural nature of Bertrand we can evaluate these expressions in any order, as long as we do not evaluate an operator until its operands become available. In other words, these expressions are actually trees that represent data-driven data-flow graphs (since they are evaluated when their operands become available), so they can be executed directly on an appropriate data-flow processor. For example, the lambda expression $\lambda x.32 + 1.8 \times x$ is precisely the data-flow graph in Figure 7.1:

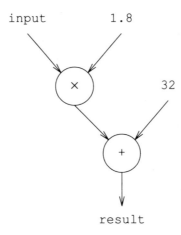

Figure 7.1   The data-flow graph for a lambda expression

Conditional expressions correspond to the data-flow "switch" operator, in Figure 7.2:

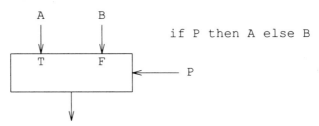

Figure 7.2   Data flow switch

Binding a value to a variable, since it obeys single-assignment semantics, corresponds to a data-flow arc from the binding operation to all operators that use that variable as input. Finally, iteration (including singly recursive rules) can be executed using streams of data-flow tokens, as demonstrated by the factorial example in Section 3.3.1.

Alternatively, expressions could be generated in the applicative intermediate form IF1 [Skedzielewski 1984]. Execution systems for IF1 exist, or are planned, on several multiprocessor systems, including the Manchester dynamic data-flow computer, the Cray-2, the HEP-1 static data-flow processor, and the DEC VAX.

The point of this section is that the procedural expressions produced by a Bertrand compiler can be executed directly on a data-flow processor. In fact, they are easier to execute on a data-flow processor than on a conventional sequential processor. The execution of a constraint program can involve many related computations that depend on each other for values in unpredictable ways. A conventional processor must keep track of these dependencies, and schedule the appropriate computation only when it has enough data to proceed. In Section 7.3 the Bertrand interpreter performed this scheduling function by waiting until the second argument of the `apply` operator became a constant. In a data-flow processor, computations proceed automatically when their data arrive, so this complicated scheduling is done by the hardware, instead of being simulated by software.

7.5 Limitations of the Equation Solver

Compilation depends on the successful conversion of relational constraint expressions into functional expressions. This conversion is performed by the equation solver, so how successful we are at compiling depends on how powerful the equation solver is. For example, consider again the electrical-circuits example from Section 5.7.

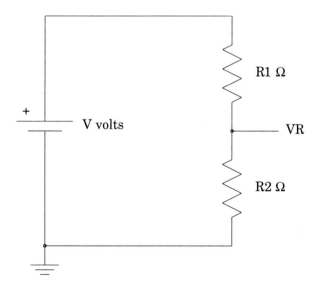

Figure 7.3   Electrical circuit for a voltage divider

This time, instead of supplying values for the voltage of the battery or for either resistor, we specify that the resistors are of equal value ($R1 = R2$), as shown in Figure 7.3, and solve for the voltage across the lower resistor (VR) in terms of the battery voltage (V). Since the resistors are of equal value, this circuit is a simple voltage divider, and VR should be one half of V.

Unfortunately, the current equation-solving rules cannot handle this problem, and so the interpreter returns the following simultaneous nonlinear equations, rewritten as far as they could be:

```
VR = current × R2;
V = 2 × current × R2;
```

When resistance values are assigned to the resistors these equations become linear and so can be solved. Without specific values for the resistors, however, the equation solver is unable to recognize that the (nonlinear) term `current × R2` occurs in both equations. If it could recognize this, it could set up the single equation

$$\frac{VR}{V} = \frac{current \times R2}{2 \times current \times R2}$$

and then cancel the variables `current` and `R2` from the numerator and denominator of the right-hand fraction.

Of course, our equation-solving rules were never meant to be a general-purpose symbolic-algebra system. When we were only interpreting our programs, these rules were generally sufficient since we normally supplied constant values for such things as the battery voltage and the resistance of the resistors. If we are compiling, however, we need to be able to solve equations containing variables without knowing their values.

If the circuit above were part of a larger circuit with the battery replaced by a signal source whose voltage varies over time, we would like to know that the voltage across the resistor is one-half the signal voltage without solving the simultaneous equations over and over for each value of the source signal. In order to do this we need more-powerful equation-solving rules that will let us compile such a resistance network. Note that more-powerful constraint-satisfaction techniques, such as relaxation, would not help at all, since relaxation works only with numeric values and cannot be used on symbolic values (such as V). Also, adding a redundant view of two resistors in series does not help.

Luckily, the literature on symbolic-algebra systems has much to offer in the way of nonlinear transformation techniques for solving equations. Techniques that use rewrite rules to solve complex polynomial equations, such as using Groebner bases [Winkler 1985], are commonly used in symbolic-algebra systems such as MACSYMA, and should be used in a system that does compilation. These techniques are slower than the current slightly nonlinear equation solver, resulting in a trade off between compile time and run time, which is to be expected. Fortunately, since our system is based on rewrite rules, advanced equation-solving techniques can be added without discarding the entire constraint-satisfaction mechanism and the existing equation solver.

Be aware, however, that nonlinear transformations are not always safe. In particular, in the example above, what if the resistance of both resistors is zero? We only specified that the two resistors were of equal resistance, so this is perfectly valid. If a resistor has no resistance, then the voltage across it is zero. Consequently the voltage across the bottom resistor must be zero, not half the battery voltage. It would be difficult to add constraints to guard against the resistance of a resistor being zero, however, since the answer to the problem above never needed to know the actual value of the resistors. We mention this problem only to point out that going to a more powerful equation solver might not be as trivial as it first seems. A human problem solver would solve the equations above, but with the implicit knowledge that if the values of the resistors are zero then all bets are off. A constraint-satisfaction system cannot be so cavalier.

Chapter 8

Conclusions

8.1 Summary and Contributions

The major contributions of this research are

- **Bertrand**, a rule-based language for specifying constraint languages and constraint-satisfaction techniques, and

- **Augmented term rewriting**, a simple inference mechanism for satisfying constraints.

Bertrand and augmented term rewriting together form a solution to the problem of specifying and generating constraint-satisfaction systems.

Bertrand is a rule-based programming language for specifying constraint-satisfaction systems. It has a simple and extensible syntax that allows expressions and equations to be treated uniformly. Bertrand also has a form of abstract data type, which allows new types of objects and operations (constraints) to be defined, even including primitives. There is no distinction between user-defined abstract data types and primitive data types, allowing a high degree of flexibility in adapting the language to specific applications.

Augmented term rewriting is a simple but powerful mechanism for implementing constraint-satisfaction systems. It is based on standard term rewriting, and inherits many valuable properties from that mechanism, most notably confluence. The extensions added to term rewriting make it expressive enough to solve a large class of constraint-satisfaction problems. Although there are more-powerful mechanisms, none are as easy to implement efficiently. For example, Horn clause logic, used as a logical basis by the programming language Prolog, is too inefficient if interpreted breadth first, and so must be executed in depth-first order. When executed depth first, Horn clause logic is incomplete, and also has a procedural semantics that would be undesirable in a constraint language.

Augmented term rewriting consists of three extensions to term rewriting: binding, objects, and types. These extensions are well integrated into term rewriting: binding can be treated as allowing new rules to be added to a term-rewriting system; objects are defined using rules; and types are defined as tags on rules. In some cases

these extensions are general replacements for specialized language features of existing term rewriters. For example, types subsume the need for qualifications on the
heads of rules as found in the Purdue Equational Interpreter. The hierarchical name
space used for objects in Bertrand unifies the concepts of local variables and structured objects so that data and procedures can be treated uniformly.

The major feature that sets augmented term rewriting apart from existing
constraint-satisfaction techniques such as propagation or relaxation is its foundation
in equational logic. This separates the problem-solving rules from the control mechanism that invokes the rules. With the formal theory of term rewriting behind it, it is
relatively simple to define the semantics of augmented term rewriting (given in
Appendix B), unlike other constraint-satisfaction techniques and languages whose
semantics have never been defined, and whose implementations tend to be ad hoc at
best.

8.2 Benefits

The benefits derived from basing a constraint language on equational logic are similar to the benefits that resulted from basing parser technology on a formal theory.
With a formal theory, parser generators were much easier to construct. In addition,
the syntax of new computer languages has become more regular. With a formal
theory, we can make our constraint languages more regular too. For example, in
most constraint languages, constraints are expressed as equations, but term-
rewriting systems operate on expressions. By treating the equal sign as a Boolean-
valued operator, we provide for a uniform treatment of equations and expressions.
This also allows our system to solve Boolean constraints, including conjunctions of
equations (higher-order constraints). Bertrand is the first constraint language to be
able either to express or solve higher-order constraints, and it did not cost anything
extra in the implementation. Treating everything as a single expression tree also
allows external programs (such as an interactive interface) to construct or manipulate constraint expressions easily.

8.2.1 Computational Completeness

Basing a constraint-satisfaction system on term rewriting also means that we inherit
computational completeness — the ability to express and compute any computable
function. This has significant advantages over other constraint languages. For
example, IDEAL required a special iterating construct for drawing dashed lines.
Other languages, such as ThingLab, have provided an "escape hatch" into their
implementation language to compute things that they cannot.

Making the constraint language itself general purpose creates a *constraint programming language*, which provides benefits similar to those provided when Horn clause logic was used to build *logic programming languages*, such as Prolog. Unlike Prolog, however, Bertrand is simple enough that it does not need to compromise its semantics to gain execution efficiency. So while in some respects Bertrand is less expressive than Prolog, it retains a nonprocedural semantics. Chapter 1 discussed some of the advantages of the declarative semantics of constraint programming languages, especially for the growing number of computer users untrained in traditional imperative computer-programming techniques. Bertrand also has features that let the user tailor a constraint programming language to a specific application.

The simplicity and generality of augmented term rewriting is also a significant advantage. The same mechanism can be used for

- Solving constraints with cycles
- Solving constraints without cycles
- Defining new data types
- Defining new constraints
- Compilation of constraints into functions
- General-purpose computation
- Symbolic computation
- Arithmetic

In existing constraint-satisfaction systems, different mechanisms are used for each of these capabilities — if they are available at all. For example, ThingLab uses local propagation to solve constraints without cycles, relaxation to solve constraints with cycles, the object-definition facilities of Smalltalk to define new data types, and machine-language primitives for arithmetic.

8.2.2 Extensibility

As shown in Chapter 4, different constraint languages have different limitations on their extensibility. Some languages, such as IDEAL, can define new structures that are like objects, but not new types of constraints (operations) on those objects. Other languages, such as Sketchpad and Juno, can define new operations on their existing data types, but cannot define new types of objects. Some languages, such as TK!Solver, are not extensible at all. In Bertrand, new objects can be defined, and constraints either can be associated with the objects, or defined as operations on those objects. Section 5.6 demonstrated how an extensible constraint language makes it easier to solve problems.

Another advantage of Bertrand is that a meaningful solution can be given even to a problem that is under-constrained. As shown in Section 5.4, the answer to a problem can be an expression (possibly containing equations) that, when true, will make the larger problem true. This allows problems to be solved as far as possible automatically, and then handed over to a human problem solver. The human problem solver can, if desired, solve only the part of the returned problem that the system could not handle, express that solution as a rule, and reenter the problem for further processing. If the rule is general enough, it can be incorporated into a library and used to solve other problems.

The only language comparable in extensibility to Bertrand is ThingLab. ThingLab borrows heavily from the Smalltalk system it was implemented in, and defines new constraints and data types using Smalltalk classes. Section 5.7 compares defining new data types and constraints using rules with an example from Section 4.1.2 showing how they are defined in ThingLab. The solution using rules is much more concise, and is also able to solve some related problems that the ThingLab solution cannot. The Bertrand solution is also more efficient computationally.

A later paper by Borning presents some extensions to ThingLab that allow the user to edit a constraint graph interactively to define new constraints, rather than requiring new constraints to be defined using Smalltalk [Borning 1985b]. This graphical interface is aided by the Smalltalk programming environment's excellent interactive-graphics facilities, but a similar interface could be applied to Bertrand. A companion report discusses defining constraints functionally [Borning 1985a], including recursive functions.

8.2.3 Efficiency

Augmented term rewriting is powerful enough to allow many constraint problems containing cycles to be solved directly, instead of using slow iterative numeric approximation techniques such as relaxation. In addition, augmented term rewriting has many properties that allow for the utilization of known techniques and optimizations for fast execution. This includes interpretation, where fast pattern-matching techniques make it possible to perform term rewriting rapidly, and compilation, using the term-rewriting system itself to generate efficient code to solve constraint problems. Augmented term rewriting also makes it easy to detect and take advantage of parallelism, opening up many new possibilities for fast computation. For example, as shown in Section 3.3.1, producer–consumer relationships are established automatically. Many enhancements to the execution speed of an augmented term-rewriting system such as Bertrand can be expressed in the language itself. For example, code optimization can be expressed as a constraint-satisfaction problem, so the code generated by a constraint-satisfaction system can even be optimized by the same system.

This book has shown that augmented term rewriting can be used to generate constraint-satisfaction systems using a rule-based specification language called Bertrand. Consequently, this language helps solve one of the major problems of constraint-satisfaction systems — their difficulty of implementation. The resulting constraint languages are both powerful and efficient.

8.3 Future Work

While the language presented by this book has been implemented, the current implementation is only an interpreter that runs on a standard sequential computer (a workstation with a graphics display). Consequently, some of the topics discussed in this book, especially those in later chapters, have not yet been "put into practice." Opportunities for interesting work abound. For example, constraint languages such as ThingLab have shown how constraint programs can be compiled into procedures. Section 7.3 discussed how such compilation could be done directly, using Bertrand itself. This would allow extremely rapid execution of constraint-language programs.

8.3.1 Parallel Execution

Implementing Bertrand on a parallel processor is another area that requires much more work. Section 7.4 discussed how this would be much easier for a language with a declarative semantics, such as Bertrand, than for a typical imperative language, but it is still far from trivial. Parallel execution would open up the possibility of even faster execution of constraint-language programs. Conversely, the problem of programming parallel processors is a research topic in its own right, which Bertrand might help solve, at least for some applications.

8.3.2 Interaction

Another useful addition to the implementation of Bertrand would be an interactive graphical front end. Constraint-satisfaction systems such as Juno and Sketchpad have demonstrated how natural such an interface is for a constraint language. Unfortunately, such interfaces are difficult to implement. A research area that might prove fruitful is to allow Bertrand to specify interface objects and constraints in the same way that it currently specifies other abstract data types. Bertrand allows new operators to be defined that operate on user-defined objects, so a natural extension would be to allow user-defined operators to be (dynamically) associated with graphical screen icons, which can then operate on graphically selected objects. For example, in Sections 3.2.2 and 6.2, we defined a rule for a `horiz` operator that constrained a line to be horizontal:

```
horiz l'line { l.begin.y = l.end.y }
```

This rule could be implemented graphically by associating the operator (horiz) with an icon (say of a horizontal T-square). If the user selected this icon and then selected a line, this would match the above rule, and constrain the line to be horizontal.

8.3.3 Multiple Solutions

The major weakness of augmented term rewriting is its inability to deal with multiple values for variables. This problem manifests itself in several different ways. For example, Bertrand is currently unable to handle default values, since overriding a default might involve assigning a new value to a variable. This problem also makes it difficult to deal with multivalued computations, such as the solution of quadratic equations. In addition, even though streams of values can be generated (using recursion), they cannot be bound to variables.

Several potential solutions to this problem are being investigated. One promising approach is to annotate bound values with a set of *assumptions*, as is done in truth-maintenance systems [Doyle 1977]. This would allow default values and multivalued computations to be handled directly. Streams could be handled by allowing (possibly infinite) streams of assumptions. The major problem with this approach is that separate copies of parts of the constraint program must be kept for each assumption set. Even ignoring streams, the number of copies can possibly grow exponentially if they are not managed carefully.

A more ambitious approach, which might be more computationally efficient is to expand the semantics of augmented term rewriting to allow streams as first-class objects. This could be done, without compromising the declarative semantics of Bertrand, by treating streams similarly to the way they are treated in Lucid [Wadge 1985]. As discussed in Section 6.3, this would also benefit input and output, which in conventional languages require the use of sideeffects, but which can be treated nonprocedurally as streams. This approach is particularly interesting since an interpreter for a subset of Lucid has been written using the Purdue Equational Interpreter [O'Donnell 1985], which can be trivially translated into Bertrand (since term rewriting is a subset of augmented term rewriting).

Once a solution to the problem of binding multiple values has been defined, Bertrand would attain the expressiveness of Horn clause logic. In addition, many other extensions would be possible. The most important would be to extend the equation solver so it can handle more-difficult problems, such as nonlinear systems of equations. One approach to this would be to implement a rule-based equation-solving method (such as using Groebner bases [Winkler 1985]), directly in Bertrand.

8.3.4 More-Powerful Equation Solvers

Another approach is to use Bertrand as a front end to a conventional symbolic-algebra system. Such an interface could be implemented so that Bertrand could use its own equation solver as much as possible, and only pass those equations on to the algebra system that are too difficult for it. The algebra system could then return the (possibly multiple) solutions to the equations, which would be further processed by Bertrand. Interfacing Bertrand to a symbolic-algebra system would also provide a much friendlier interface to these systems. For example, geometric theorems could be expressed as a set of constraints, instead of forcing the user to translate them manually into equations to be solved.

Other potential extensions to the equation solver include the ability to deal with inequalities. For example, the constraints "$x \geq 5$" and "$x \leq 5$" should constrain the value of x to be 5. We would also like to be able to constrain a number to be an integer. Such extensions need to be made carefully, however, to keep them from slowing down the entire system.

8.3.5 Data Types

Another interesting research area is abstract data types. Term-rewriting systems, such as the Purdue Equational Interpreter, typically use unevaluated terms for data types (as does Prolog). For example, the point (5, 3) might be represented as the term `point(5,3)`. Augmented term rewriting allows data types to be represented this way, but it supplies an additional, incompatible, representation. For example, in Section 3.2.3, a point could be created using the rule

```
aPoint { x: aNumber ; y: aNumber ; true } 'point
```

As discussed in Section 7.1.3, both representations have their advantages. The main advantage of using unevaluated terms for data types is notational — elements of data types can be selected by position. This suggests that some notation to define selectors on elements of Bertrand's abstract data types would solve this problem.

8.3.6 Acceptability of Nonprocedural Languages

Finally, one of the strengths of Bertrand, its nonprocedural semantics, is also one of its main weaknesses. Programmers are not accustomed to nonprocedural languages, and often resist using them. It is hoped that this prejudice on the part of programmers can be overcome by using Bertrand to implement constraint languages, where procedural information is the exception rather than the rule. Until these prejudices can be overcome, however, this will tend to limit the potential use of Bertrand to descriptive tasks such as graphics and modeling, but these are rich fields, with many interesting problems.

Alternatively, procedural constructs could be added to Bertrand to improve its efficiency on sequential processors. For example, we could easily add operators that control when their arguments are to be evaluated. This would allow conditional operators (if/then/else) to wait until their predicate expression evaluates to either true or false before other arguments are evaluated. Similar restrictions could help the performance of other operators.

Libraries and Examples

Bertrand is normally used in conjunction with one or more libraries of rules. This appendix discusses these libraries and gives examples of their use. All of the examples have been run using the current Bertrand implementation.

A.1 BEEP

BEEP is the Bertrand Elementary Equation Processor, the equation solver used in this document. BEEP defines rules for the following operators, listed in order of increasing precedence.

Category	Operator	Description	Associativity
Statement	;	assert	right
Expression	,	list	right
Logical	->	implication	right
	|	Boolean or	left
	~ |	nor	left
	&	Boolean and	left
	~ &	nand	left
	~	Boolean not	prefix
Relational	=	equality	nonassociative
	~ =	inequality	nonassociative
	>	greater than	nonassociative
	>=	greater or equal	nonassociative
	<	less than	nonassociative
	<=	less or equal	nonassociative
Arithmetic	+	addition	left
	−	subtraction	left
	⋆	multiplication	left
	/	division	left
	trunc	integer part	prefix
	abs	absolute value	prefix

	sin	sine	prefix
	cos	cosine	prefix
	tan	tangent	prefix
	atan	arc tangent	prefix
	^	exponentiation	nonassociative
	–	unary minus	prefix
Constants	true	Boolean	nullary
	false	Boolean	nullary
	nil	distinguished value	nullary
Typed object	aNumber	declare a number	nullary

BEEP also uses the following types

'nonzero	any numeric constant except 0
'constant	numeric constant
'linear	constant or linear expression
'expression	any expression that is not linear or a constant
'number	any of the above

The type 'linear is a supertype of 'constant, and 'constant is a supertype of 'nonzero. This means that any rule that will match a linear expression will also match a constant, *unless* there is another rule that only matches a constant, and so on. Type 'number is a supertype of 'linear and 'expression.

The following is the complete set of rules for BEEP. An ellipsis (...) introduces a comment that runs to the end of the line.

```
            ... semicolon patterns
true ; a                                    {a}
(a; b) ; c                                  {a; b; c}
(a & b) ;  c                                {a; b; c}
            ... Boolean patterns
a -> b                                      { ~ (a & ~b) }
a ~& b                                      { ~ (a & b) }
a  | b                                      { ~ (~a & ~b) }
a ~| b                                      { ~a & ~b}
false & a                                   {false}
true & a                                    {a}
~true                                       {false}
~false                                      {true}
~ ~a                                        {a}
```

```
              ... relational patterns
a  ~= b                                    { ~ (a = b) }
a > b                                      {b < a}
a >= b                                     {b <= a}
          ... simple algebra
a'constant = b ^ c'constant                {a ^ (1/c) = b}
a'linear = b'linear + c'expression         {a - b = c}
a'linear = b'constant * c'expression       {a / b = c}
a'constant = b / c                         {c ~= 0; b/a = c}
0 / b                                      {b ~= 0; 0}
0 * b                                      {0}
a'linear ^ 0                               {a ~= 0; 1}
a'expression ^ 0                           {a ~= 0; 1}
a'linear ^ 1                               {a}
a'expression ^ 1                           {a}
          ... standard form
a'expression = b'linear                    {b = a}
a'expression + b'linear                    {b + a}
a'expression - b'linear                    { (-b) + a}
a'expression * b'linear                    {b * a}
a'linear * b'constant                      {b * a}
a'linear = b'linear                        {0 = b - a}
a'nonzero = b'linear ; c                   {0 = b - a; c}
          ... builtin
0 = b'linear ;   c                         {$solve}
a'linear + b'linear                        {$add}
a'linear - b'linear                        {$sub}
a'linear * b'constant                      {$mul}
a'linear / b'constant                      {$div}
- a'linear                                 {$neg}
a'constant = b'constant                    {$eq}
a'constant < b'constant                    {$lt}
a'constant <= b'constant                   {$le}
a'constant ^ b'constant                    {$exp}
trunc b'constant                           {$floor}
abs b'constant                             {$abs}
sin b'constant                             {$sin}
cos b'constant                             {$cos}
tan b'constant                             {$tan}
atan b'constant                            {$atan}
```

Any operator that begins with a dollar sign ($) is a primitive. The $solve operator, like the others, is a primitive for efficiency reasons (see Section 5.1 for a version of $solve written in Bertrand). As discussed in Section 3.1.1, all primitives could (at least conceptually) be written as rules.

Most of these rules are fairly intuitive — things like "not false is replaced by true" and so on. Also note that the rules for dealing with division (under the comment ... `simple algebra`) add constraints to make sure that denominators do not vanish. Other rules deal with getting constants near each other so arithmetic can be done on them. These rules use the commutative and associative laws, but in order to prevent infinite loops we cannot include rules such as

```
a + b { b + a }
```

Instead, the second rule under the comment ... `standard form` moves constants to the left. By moving constants in the same direction, eventually they will find each other so that arithmetic can be performed on them.

A.1.1 Factorial

In Section 3.3.1 we defined some rules that evaluated the factorial function of n as the product of the first n integers, which is a nonstandard way of defining factorial. We did it that way because it better showed the pipelining automatically set up by Bertrand. We can, of course, define a more conventional factorial:

```
fact 1 { 1 }
fact n'constant { n × fact(n−1) }
```

Like the other version, Bertrand automatically sets up a stream between the producer of the list of values (the `fact` rule) and the consumer (the multiplication), using the associative law of multiplication. This program is also simple enough to show the tree at every step of the rewriting: A complete trace of the execution of `fact 5` (produced by the Bertrand tracer) is

```
fact 5
5 × (fact(5 − 1))
5 × fact 4
5 × (4 × fact(4 − 1))
(5 × 4) × fact(4 − 1)
20 × fact(4 − 1)
20 × fact(3)
20 × (3 × fact(3 − 1))
(20 × 3) × fact(3 − 1)
60 × fact(3 − 1)
60 × fact(2)
60 × (2 × fact(2 − 1))
(60 × 2) × fact(2 − 1)
120 × fact(2 − 1)
120 × fact(1)
120 × 1
120
```

A.1.2 Simultaneous Equations

Here is a set of simultaneous equations from a textbook on linear algebra:

```
main {
     4.6237×a + 2.6914×b - 3.7517×c = 1.4023;
    -2.4037×a + 1.0432×b + 0.7589×c = 0.3724;
     1.0462×a + 2.0495×b + 6.3524×c = -2.4728;
    a, b, c
    }
```

Bertrand produces the (correct) answer:

```
-.188747 , .23866 , -.435184
```

with 18 rule rewritings and 23 calls to primitive arithmetic routines, in 0.15 second.

A.1.3 Triangle Equality

Here is an example of a simple quadratic equation that can be solved by the above rules:

```
main {
    c^2 = a^2 + b^2; a = 3; c = 5; b
    }
```

The answer returned is 4.

Note, however, that only the positive root is returned. This is a result of the rule

```
a'constant = b ^ c'constant    {a ^ (1/c) = b}
```

in the equation solver. This rule causes the expression

```
16 = b^2
```

which has two possible solutions, to be rewritten into

```
16 ^ (1/2) = b
```

which has only one solution. Since, as discussed in Section 3.3.2, the current version of Bertrand cannot bind multiple values to a variable, there is no easy way to avoid this problem. This problem also occurs in the rule that calls the primitive operator $atan, since it only returns a single value.

A.1.4 More Word Problems

Here is a slightly more challenging problem. I have 25 coins in my pocket, nickels, dimes, and quarters. They are worth $3.45. I have 7 more nickels than dimes. How many coins of each type do I have? If we write this problem out as Bertrand program, it looks like this:

```
main {
    nickels: aNumber;
    dimes: aNumber;
    quarters: aNumber;
    nickels + dimes + quarters = 25;
    nickels×5 + dimes×10 + quarters×25 = 345;
    dimes = 7 + nickels;
    nickels, dimes, quarters
    }
```

The answer returned is 5 nickels, 12 dimes, and 8 quarters.

If (for some unimaginable reason) we were going to solve a lot of problems of this type, we might want to define some data types to help us make the program look more like the problem statement. We define a postfix operator `coins` that creates a set of coins of a certain value, and a postfix `cent` operator, for syntactic sugar.

```
value′number coins {
    total: aNumber;
    value: aNumber;
    num: aNumber;
    total = value×num
    } ′money

n cent { n / 100 }

main {
    nickels: 5 cent coins;
    dimes: 10 cent coins;
    quarters: 25 cent coins;

    nickels.num + dimes.num + quarters.num = 25;
    nickels.total + dimes.total + quarters.total = 3.45;
    dimes.num = 7 + nickels.num;
    nickels.num, dimes.num, quarters.num
    }
```

This example shows how a rule for creating an object can be parameterized, in this case with the value of the coin. Of course, we get the same answer.

A.1.5 Temperatures

And last, but not least, here is the temperature-conversion program written in Bertrand:

```
F = 32 + 9/5×C
```

What could be simpler?

We can also define operators for different units of temperature measurement. For example, we can define rules for the postfix operators `Celsius`, `Fahrenheit`, and `Kelvin`, and one for a postfix `degrees` operator, purely for syntactic sugar:

```
n Celsius { n }
n Fahrenheit { (n − 32) × (5/9) }
n Kelvin { n − 273 }
n degrees { n }
```

We are using Celsius as our reference unit. We can then write programs asking questions like

```
main { x: aNumber;
    0 degrees Kelvin = x degrees Fahrenheit;
    x
    }
```

This program solves for the value of x in degrees Fahrenheit that is equal to zero degrees Kelvin (−459.4 degrees Fahrenheit). Since we can solve simultaneous equations, we also can ask questions such as

```
main { x: aNumber;
    x degrees Celsius = x degrees Fahrenheit;
    x
    }
```

and get the answer −40, since −40 degrees Celsius is the same temperature as −40 degrees Fahrenheit.

A.2 BAG

BAG is the Bertrand Archetype Graphics library.* It defines the types 'point and
'line, and provides access to graphical primitives for drawing lines, circles, and
strings at specified locations. These rules use two special character operators beyond
those supplied by BEEP, the infix at sign (@) used to create new points, and the bang
(!) operator, both postfix and infix, used to draw graphic objects. These rules provide
only rudimentary support for graphics — most programs define further rules.

```
          ... points
aPoint                      { x: aNumber; y: aNumber; true } 'point
x @ y                       { p: aPoint; p.x = x; p.y = y; p }
p'point = q'point           { p.x=q.x & p.y=q.y }
p'point + q'point           { p.x+q.x @ p.y+q.y }


          ... lines
aLine                       { begin: aPoint; end: aPoint; true } 'line
l'line !                    { ((l.begin.x,l.begin.y),
                              (l.end.x,l.end.y)) ! }
horiz l'line                { l.begin.y = l.end.y }
vert l'line                 { l.begin.x = l.end.x }
l1'line conn l2'line        { l1.end = l2.begin }
widthof l'line              { l.end.x - l.begin.x }
heightof l'line             { l.begin.y - l.end.y }


          ... draw primitives
(a'constant, (x'constant, y'constant)) !
          {$drawnum}
((x1'constant, y1'constant),(x2'constant, y2'constant)) !
          {$drawline}
(a'string, (x'constant, y'constant)) !
          {$drawstr}


          ... mouse primitives
mousex                {$mousex}   ... x coordinate of mouse
mousey                {$mousey}   ... y coordinate of mouse
mouseb                {$mouseb}   ... mouse buttons
```

---

* After this one, I think I will give up trying to give libraries acronyms starting with the letter B.

A.2.1 Diagrams

Here are some additional diagrams, drawn using the rules defined in Section 6.2.1. Since the rules are defined elsewhere, we will only show the constraint program for each diagram.

The following program:

```
main {
        user: circle "user";
        gin: box "graphic input";
        bertrand: box "Bertrand";
        database: box "database";
        gout: box "frame buffer";
        display: circle "display";
        app: box "applications";
        user.left = 100; user.top = 80;

        user rightto gin; gin rightto bertrand;
        bertrand downto database; database upto bertrand;
        bertrand rightto gout; gout rightto display;
        database rightto app;
        true
        }
```

produces the following diagram:

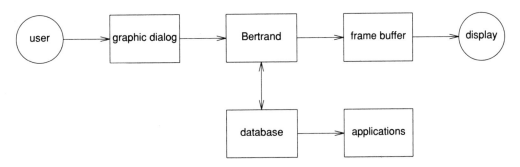

This diagram shows how a constraint language built with Bertrand would fit into a design system (such as for ME-CAD). The user interacts with the system through an interface, called "graphic dialog," giving the system constraints on the design. These constraints are satisfied by Bertrand, which draws the resulting figures in a graphic output device, a "frame buffer." Information about specific designs is stored in a database — this database can also be accessed by other application programs.

A slight change to the program, and we get a different diagram, this time with a "cycle":

```
main {
        user: circle "user";
        gin: box "graphic input";
        dialog: box "graphic dialog";     new gob
        bertrand: box "Bertrand";
        database: circle "database";
        gout: box "frame buffer";
        display: circle "display";
        app: box "applications";
        display.left = 100; display.top = 80;

        user rightto gin;
        gin rightto dialog;
        dialog upto bertrand;
        bertrand rightto database;
        database leftto bertrand;
        bertrand leftto gout;
        gout leftto display;
        display downto user;
        database rightto app;
        true
        }
```

This cycle is not like a cycle in a constraint graph, since it corresponds to the constraint problem being overconstrained. The position of the box "graphic dialog" is fixed relative to both "Bertrand" and "graphic input," which in turn are fixed relative to each other. Since these constraints do not contradict each other, they are merely redundant, and do not cause any problems.

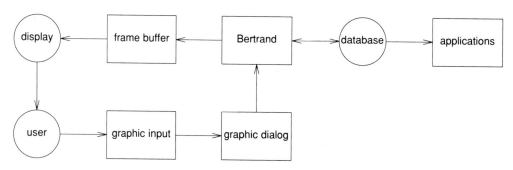

A.2.2 Graphics Applications

The following pages contain examples of output that are meant to be evocative of different graphical applications of constraint languages, including mapping and mechanical design [Leler 1985]. They have all been produced using Bertrand.

Mechanical Design

The following pictures are sketches for a plug and socket. The plug and socket are the same data type, with similar topologies, but with different dimensions.

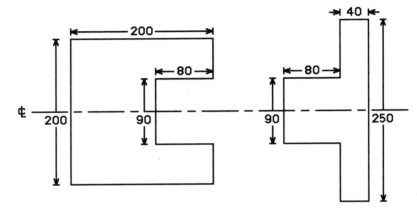

The mating parts of the plug and socket are constrained to be the same size.

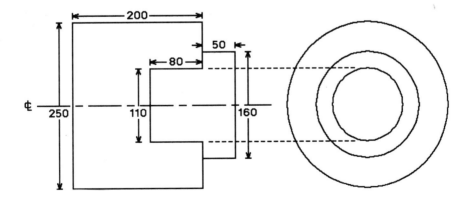

We also use constraints to arrange objects in the drawing relative to each other, so that when one object is moved, the others move to maintain their proper relative positions.

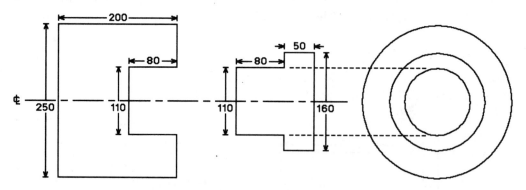

Mapping

This example shows a map constrained to lie within a certain rectangle.

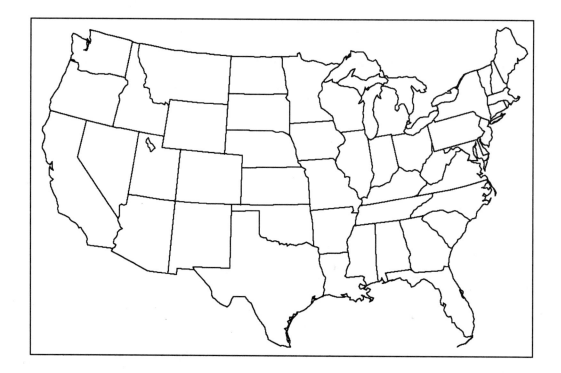

We can stretch maps arbitrarily, including constraining the right side of the map to be to the left of the left side, or the top to be below the bottom, as in the following picture.

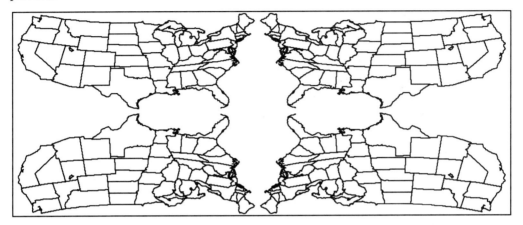

Operational Semantics

This appendix presents an operational semantics for augmented term rewriting, using the functional notation of denotational semantics. One of the advantages of term rewriting (augmented or not) is that the rewritings can be interpreted as purely syntactic transformations, without regard to any meaning that might be attached to the symbols being transformed. Consequently, a full denotational semantics is not required.

The semantics of augmented term rewriting are presented incrementally, using the same order as Chapter 3. Initially we ignore types (guards and tags) and then reintroduce them later. Finally, Section B.5 discusses some of the properties of augmented term-rewriting systems, including soundness and confluence. Readers who are only mildly interested in semantics might still want to read this final section.

Notation

In this appendix, as in the rest of the book, program fragments and other syntactic entities will be written using a typewriter-style `Courier` font. In addition, this appendix uses several other fonts to distinguish different types of variables and constants. Syntactic domains will be written using the Helvetica font, with the first letter in upper case. Elements of syntactic domains are also in Helvetica, but in all lower case. For example, Number is the syntactic domain of all numeric constants, and number represents a specific element of that domain, perhaps the specific constant `3.14159`.

Semantic domains are written in the same manner as syntactic domains, using Helvetica font with the first letter capitalized, but elements of semantic domains are represented by single letters. Elements of semantic domains are typically functions; if these functions perform transformations over syntactic domains they are written using a single, Helvetica lower-case letter. More complicated syntactic functions, which typically perform transformations over semantic domains, are written using a single, bold Helvetica upper-case letter.

Following standard convention, our semantic functions will use a notation where syntactic entities are enclosed in double square brackets ($[\![\ ]\!]$). Function application is indicated by simple juxtaposition, with parentheses used only for disambiguation. For example,

F (x $[\![$ v $]\!]$) y

applies the function **F** to two arguments: the result of applying the function x to the syntactic name v, and y.

Objects that are not explicitly taken from any domain will be written using **bold** lower-case letters. These objects include simple syntactic functions, such as the **concat** function that performs simple string concatenation on syntactic objects, and keywords such as **if**, and **then**.

B.1 Syntax

In order to concentrate on the semantics we will introduce a greatly simplified version of the Bertrand syntax. Expressions are written using a functional notation, and operators are only allowed to be names. For example, the Bertrand expression

```
3 + 4 = 7
```

would be written as

```
eq(plus(3, 4), 7)
```

Our syntactic domains are as follows:

> Name = domain of names, with element name
> Number = domain of numbers, with element number
> Var = domain of variables, with element var
> Exp = domain of expressions, with element exp
> Rule = domain of rules, with element rule
> Prog = domain of sets of rules, with element prog
> Op = domain of operators, with element op

An element name of Name is taken from the normal domain of identifiers, which are alphanumeric strings that begin with an alphabetical character. An element number of Number is a string of numeric digits, possibly containing a single decimal point, indicating a numeric constant.

The following syntactic description is given in tabular form, rather than using Backus–Naur Form, so there is no meta-notation. The seven special characters " } {) (. : " and " , " are part of the language syntax.

Table B.1		
A	*is a*	*or a*
prog	rule	rule prog
rule	exp { exp }	
exp	labeled_exp	simple_exp
labeled_exp	var : opterm	
simple_exp	cterm	opterm
cterm	var	number
opterm	op ( )	op (args)
op	name	
args	arg	arg, args
arg	exp	
var	name	name . var

A prog (program) is a set of rules, and a rule is a directed (ordered) pair of expressions. We define two syntactic functions **head** and **body**, which, when applied to a rule, return the first and second expressions of the rule, respectively.

> **head**: Rule → Exp
> **body**: Rule → Exp

For simplicity, labels are not explicitly prohibited in the heads of rules, but they will be ignored. Nullary operators have an empty argument list, but the parentheses are still necessary, for example, `nil()`. Numbers are also considered to be nullary operators, but do not need the trailing parentheses. The following names are reserved:

> root   true   is   Label   untyped

They can only be used in special ways, which will be outlined below.

As indicated in the table, a var (variable name) can be either a single name or a compound name (two or more names separated by periods). Without losing generality, we can restrict variable names in the heads of rules (parameters) to single names. To manipulate compound names we define the syntactic functions **concat**, **first**, and **rest**.

> **concat**: (Var × Var) → Var
> **first**: Var → Var
> **rest**: Var → Var

The **concat** function takes two variable names as arguments, and concatenates them, separated by a period. The function **first** returns the first name of a compound name, **rest** returns the rest of the name (minus the period). For example,

concat aaa bbb → aaa.bbb
first aaa.bbb → aaa
rest aaa.bbb.ccc → bbb.ccc

B.2 Semantics

Our semantics will use the following domains:

NameSpace = Var → Exp
Global = NameSpace
Param = NameSpace

An element n of NameSpace is a function that maps a variable to its value, which is an expression. We also define the function **bound**, which, when applied to a NameSpace and a Var, returns true if the variable is bound in the name space, and false otherwise. The distinguished name space φ is the **empty name space**, where "**bound** φ var" is false for all variables. Name spaces are used for two purposes: the Global name space stores the values of the global variables across an entire program's execution, and the Param name space stores the values of the parameter variables for each rule invocation. An element p of Param is the name space that holds the values for the parameter variables in the head of a rule when the rule matches a redex.

New values are added to name spaces using the standard update function [/]. For example, the expression

n [var / exp]

returns a new name space that is identical to the name space n, except that the variable var has as its value the expression exp. We also define a function **instantiate** that takes a name space and an expression and returns an expression; each variable in the expression that also occurs in the name space is replaced (in the expression) by its value.

instantiate: (NameSpace × Exp) → Exp

For example,

instantiate (φ [⟦ x ⟧ / ⟦ 5 ⟧]) ⟦ eq(plus(x,0),x) ⟧ → ⟦ eq(plus(5,0),5) ⟧

We also define a semantic domain called State:

State = Exp × Global

An element s of State is a pair that consists of an expression, called the **subject expression**, and a name space, called the **global name space**.

The semantic function **T** maps a program into a function that transforms a state, called the **initial** State, into a new state, called the **terminal** State (by a sequence of rewritings):

$$\textbf{T}\colon \mathsf{Prog} \rightarrow (\mathsf{State} \rightarrow \mathsf{State})$$

The initial state is a pair that consists of the initial subject expression

```
root: main()
```

and the empty name space ϕ. The variable name `root` is reserved, and can never be used as a label for any expression other than in the initial state. Since the initial state is a constant, **T** can be regarded as a function that maps a program into a (terminal) state.

$$\textbf{T}\colon \mathsf{Prog} \rightarrow \mathsf{State}$$

B.2.1 Standard Term Rewriting

First we will give the semantics for a standard term-rewriting system in terms of the semantic functions **T** and **R**. The function **T** is defined as a term-rewriting system. Term rewriting has been covered formally elsewhere [O'Donnell 1977] (see also Section 3.1, and the executable semantics in Appendix C). A standard term-rewriting system takes an initial subject expression exp_0, and a set of rules, and defines a sequence of expressions

$$\mathsf{exp}_0 \rightarrow \mathsf{exp}_1 \rightarrow \ldots \rightarrow \mathsf{exp}_n$$

Each arrow ($\rightarrow$) indicates a **single rewriting** of the subject expression exp_i, which produces a new subject expression exp_{i+1}. In order to be able to name subexpressions we introduce the notation

$$\mathsf{exp}_i \, @ \, \xi$$

which denotes a subexpression of exp_i at occurrence ξ. An **occurrence** is simply a location inside an expression. For example, an occurrence could be represented as a sequence of directions to follow from the root of the expression tree to arrive at a specific subexpression tree. A single rewriting occurs if there exists a parameter name space p, such that for some rule rule_k, p contains the substitutions for all the variables in **head** rule_k to make it exactly equivalent to $\mathsf{exp}_i \, @ \, \xi$. In other words, a single rewriting occurs if the head of some rule matches a subexpression of the subject expression. If an appropriate rule_k and p are found for exp_i, then the new subject expression is defined by

$$\mathsf{exp}_{i+1} = \mathsf{exp}_i \, @ \, \xi \leftarrow \textbf{R} \, \mathsf{rule}_k \, \mathsf{p}$$

where $\exp_i @ \xi \leftarrow \mathbf{R}\ \text{rule}_k\ p$ denotes the expression obtained by replacing the sub-expression of $\exp_i$ at occurrence ξ by the expression $\mathbf{R}\ \text{rule}_k\ p$, defined by the function $\mathbf{R}$. The semantic function $\mathbf{R}$ takes a rule and a parameter name space, and returns a new expression

$$\mathbf{R}: (\ \text{Rule} \times \text{Param}\ ) \rightarrow \text{Exp}$$

The resulting expression is the body of the rule with all of its variables replaced by their values from the parameter name space p:

$$\mathbf{R}\ \text{rule}\ p = \mathbf{instantiate}\ p\ (\mathbf{body}\ \text{rule}\ )$$

For example, if the set of rules contains the single rule

```
op (op (X) )  {  op (X)  }
```

and the initial subject expression is

```
op (op (op (op (5) ) ) )
```

then a standard term-rewriting system can match the (single) rule at the outermost term of the subject expression, with the parameter name space p equal to

$$\phi\ [\ [\![\ X\ ]\!]\ /\ [\![\ \text{op (op (5))}\ ]\!]\ ]$$

The outermost term of the subject expression (the entire subject expression) is replaced by the body of the rule, `op (X)`, with `X` replaced by its value, resulting in the expression

```
op (op (op (5) ) )
```

This process repeats, producing the following sequence of expressions:

$$\text{op (op (op (op (5))))} \rightarrow \text{op (op (op (5)))} \rightarrow \text{op (op (5))} \rightarrow \text{op (5)}$$

Note that the initial subject expression above contains three different redexes. In cases such as this, where more than one subexpression of the subject expression matches the head of one or more rules in prog, the order in which they are rewritten is undefined (they can be done in any order). When there are no more rewritings to be done, the system terminates and returns the final expression in the sequence. If the system does not terminate, the result is undefined (equal to **bottom**).

B.2.2 Augmented Term Rewriting

Instead of the sequence of expressions defined by a standard term-rewriting system, an **augmented term-rewriting system** defines a sequence of states. Each state s_i consists of a subject expression $\exp_i$, and a global name space g_i.

$$(\exp_0 \times g_0) \rightarrow (\exp_1 \times g_1) \rightarrow \ \dots\ \rightarrow (\exp_n \times g_n)$$

Each single rewriting can modify the expression or the global name space or both. A single rewriting can be done in one of three ways:

1) By binding a value to an unbound variable in the global name space.

2) By replacing a bound variable in the subject expression by its value.

3) By matching a redex of the subject expression to the head of a rule in prog, and replacing the redex by the body of the rule, as in standard term rewriting.

The rules in prog perform only the third type of rewriting; in order to perform the other two types of rewriting we implicitly add two "rules," which we will call Λ and Γ, to every prog.

The rule Λ, corresponding to the first type of rewriting, behaves as if it were written as the rule

```
is(V, E)  { true() }
```

that matches a binary operator named is. The actual parameters to is must be a variable $\hat{v}$ (from the domain var) that is not bound in the global name space, and an expression $\hat{e}$ (from the domain exp). The rule Λ also has a side effect, namely, it modifies the global name space by binding the expression $\hat{e}$ as the value of $\hat{v}$.

The rule Γ, corresponding to the second type of rewriting, behaves as if it were written as the rule:

```
V { E }
```

whose head can only match bound variables. This rule actually represents a set of rules of the form:

```
v̂ { ê }
```

whose heads are atoms in the global name space (bound variables), and whose bodies are the corresponding values of the variables in the global name space g. These rules replace bound variables by their values.

The augmented term rewriter **T** performs a sequence of rewritings (of one of the three types above) producing a sequence of states. As in a standard term-rewriting system, for each single rewriting (of whichever type), **T** finds a subexpression of the subject expression, $exp_i @ \xi$ that matches the head of some rule $rule_k$ (including Λ and Γ), using substitution function p. **T** then replaces this subexpression with a new expression, defined by **R**. For a standard term-rewriting system **R** took a rule and a parameter name space, and returned an expression. For an augmented term-rewriting system, **R** also takes a global name space, and transforms it into a new global name space, which, combined with the new subject expression, forms the new state.

$$\mathbf{R}: (\text{ Rule} \times \text{Param} \times \text{Global }) \rightarrow (\text{ Exp} \times \text{Global })$$

In a standard term-rewriting system the function **R** only replaced the parameter variables in the body of a rule by their values. In an augmented term-rewriting system the transformations are slightly more complex. We will define **R** by enumeration, depending on the type of rewriting that is being done.

1) For the first type of rewriting, the "rule" that was matched is Λ:

```
is(V, E) { true() }
```

so the parameter name space (p) contains parameter bindings for V and E. In this case, **R** is

$$\mathbf{R} \llbracket \text{ is}(V, E) \ \{ \ \text{true}() \ \} \ \rrbracket \ p \ g =$$
$$\textbf{if bound } g \ (\ p \llbracket V \rrbracket \ ) \textbf{ then error}$$
$$\textbf{else} \ \llbracket \text{true}() \ \rrbracket, \ g \ [\ p \llbracket V \rrbracket / p \llbracket E \rrbracket \ ]$$

The update function $g \ [\ p \llbracket V \rrbracket / p \llbracket E \rrbracket \ ]$ updates g (the global name space) by binding the variable bound to V in the parameter name space to the expression bound to E in the parameter name space. If the name is already bound, then an **error** is returned to the term rewriter **T**, which can simply print a message and halt. The meaning of the syntactic constant `true()` is the Boolean truth value true.

An example of how this rule is used is the expression

```
is(x, 5)
```

This expression matches the rule Λ, binding the variable name x to V and 5 to E in the parameter name space p. The semantic function to be evaluated is

$$\textbf{if bound } g \ (\ p \llbracket V \rrbracket \ ) \textbf{ then error}$$
$$\textbf{else} \ \llbracket \text{true}() \ \rrbracket, g \ [\ p \llbracket V \rrbracket / p \llbracket E \rrbracket \ ]$$

Assuming x is unbound in g, the result of this evaluation is

$$\llbracket \text{true}() \ \rrbracket, g \ [\ \llbracket x \rrbracket / \llbracket 5 \rrbracket \ ]$$

consisting of a new expression `true()` to be inserted back into the subject expression, and a new global name space, where the value of x is 5.

2) For the case where the rule matched is Γ, the redex is a bound variable and the parameter name space p contains the single name V, whose value is the bound variable. **R** is

$$\mathbf{R} \llbracket \ V \ \{ \ E \ \} \ \rrbracket \ p \ g = g \ p \llbracket V \rrbracket, g$$

In this case, we simply replace the name of the bound variable with its value. The global name space (g) is unchanged.

For example, if the global name space has the value 5 for the variable x (perhaps because of the example above), then in the expression

```
plus(x, 1)
```

the variable x will match the rule Γ, binding the name x to V in the parameter name space p. The semantic function **R** trivially evaluates to

⟦ 5 ⟧, g

The term rewriting function **T** will replace the bound variable x with the syntactic constant 5 in the subject expression, resulting in the expression

```
plus(5, 1)
```

The global name space (g) is unchanged.

3) The last case is the standard one, where the redex matched the head of some rule in prog. As well as containing the bindings for the parameters, the parameter name space (p) also contains the variable Label, whose value is the label of the redex. If the redex was unlabeled, we assume that some unique name is bound to the variable Label. We will omit the details of how unique label names for unlabeled redexes are generated, but we will assume that it is done in a functional manner, of course. For details on how this might be done see the executable semantics in Appendix C. **R** is

R rule p g = (**atr-instantiate** p (**body** rule)), g

As in the last case, the global name space g is unchanged; in this case it is also unused.

In a standard term-rewriting system the new subject expression was formed by replacing the parameter variables in the body of the rule by their values, using the **instantiate** function. In an augmented term-rewriting system, however, variables in the body of a rule are not necessarily all parameter variables, so we must slightly redefine the **instantiate** function. The **atr-instantiate** function takes a name space p and an expression, and replaces each variable var in the expression by the result of evaluating

if bound (p var)
    then p var
    else concat (p ⟦ Label ⟧) var

As for the **instantiate** function, **atr-instantiate** replaces all variables found in the (parameter) name space by their values. In addition, variables not found in the name space are prefixed, using the **concat** function, by the value of the name Label.

For example, let us apply the rule

```
op1(Q) { op2(5, Q, y) }
```

to the subexpression

```
lab: op1(m)
```

The global name space is unchanged (and unused), and the parameter name space (p) contains the name Q, whose value is m, and Label, whose value is lab. The new expression is generated from the body of the rule by replacing parameter variables by their values, and prefixing all other names with the label name. The variable Q is a parameter, so it is replaced by its value (m), and the variable y is prefixed with the label (lab). The resulting expression is

```
op2(5, m, lab.y)
```

Recall that in an augmented term-rewriting system a variable name can be a compound name (two or more names separated by periods). The **atr-instantiate** function treats compound names slightly differently — each compound name is replaced by the result of evaluating

if bound p (**first** var)
      then concat (p (**first** var)) (**rest** var)
      else concat (p ⟦ Label ⟧) var

Because of our earlier restriction that parameter variables cannot be compound names, an entire compound variable cannot be a parameter, but its first name can be. In this case, the leading parameter name is replaced by its value. If the initial name of a compound variable is not a parameter, it is prefixed by the label name, as before. For example, the rule

```
old(X) { gt(X.age, 70) }
```

applied to the expression

```
old(president)
```

results in the expression

```
gt(president.age, 70)
```

B.3 Adding Types: Tags and Guards

Adding types does not change the semantics that much. The syntax of our language is extended as shown in Table B.2. In addition to their old form, a type name (tag) can optionally be appended to a rule. Variables in the head of a rule (parameters) can also be followed by a type (a guard).

Table B.2	
A	*is (also) a*
rule	exp { exp } type
var	name type
type	′ name

Type names are distinguished from other names by prefixing them with a single quote (′). Variables can now have a type, as well as a value. The semantic domains must be changed as follows:

$$\text{State} = \text{Exp} \times \text{Global} \times \text{TypeSpace}$$
$$\text{TypeSpace} = \text{Var} \rightarrow \text{Type}$$

A TypeSpace is similar to a NameSpace, and uses the same update function. The function **R** now also takes a TypeSpace t, and returns a new TypeSpace (as part of the returned state):

$$\textbf{R}: (\text{ Rule} \times \text{Param} \times \text{Global} \times \text{TypeSpace }) \rightarrow (\text{ Exp} \times \text{Global} \times \text{TypeSpace })$$

The first two cases of **R** (for rules Λ and Γ) just pass the type space through unchanged. The remaining case of **R** (for normal term rewriting) is

$$\textbf{R} \text{ rule p g t} = (\textbf{atr-instantiate } \text{p} (\textbf{body } \text{rule})), \text{g}, \text{t} [\text{ p} [\![\text{Label}]\!] / \textbf{tag } \text{rule}]$$

The TypeSpace t is updated by giving the label of the redex (the variable p $[\![$ Label $]\!]$) the type of the tag of rule. The function **tag** returns the tag of a rule. If the rule has no tag, then **tag** returns the reserved type ′untyped.

Lastly, we need to change the matching function of the term-rewriting system **T** so that a parameter in the head of a rule that has a guard can only match a variable of the correct type. By correct type, we mean the same type or a subtype.

B.4 Differences

The differences between Bertrand and the language formally defined above are mainly syntactic. The above language used parentheses to distinguish between operators and variables. In Bertrand, operator names can be used in binary infix and unary prefix, postfix, or outfix notation, so they must be distinguished explicitly from variable names. This is accomplished by operator definitions, which also serve to declare an operator's arity, associativity, and precedence (see Section 3.3). Also, Bertrand allows many special characters to be used as operators.

Bertrand also allows global variables, which are variable names in the body of a rule that begin with a period. These are treated like local variables, except that they are *not* prefixed with the label name when the rule is instantiated. We also eliminate the reserved name `root` and just use the period as the root of the name space. Consequently, a local variable x of the `main` rule becomes `.x` instead of `root.x`. Bertrand also eliminates the other reserved syntactic variables and constants (such as `Label`), except for the single reserved operator `is`.

Lastly, Bertrand requires all free variables (bindable atoms) to be typed by using them as a label of a redex. This is equivalent to requiring variables to be declared in a conventional programming language. If a labeled subexpression matches a rule that has no tag, then the label variable is of type `'untyped`, as before. Bertrand treats `'untyped` as a valid type. If a free variable never occurs as the label of a redex, then it is undeclared, and has no type (not even `'untyped`). An undeclared free variable is treated as an error.

B.5 Discussion

This section discusses some of the properties of augmented term-rewriting systems. As in our semantics above, we will concentrate on the differences between augmented term rewriting and standard term rewriting.

In a standard term-rewriting system, if the similarity relation between the head and body of each rule is equality (the rules are *sound*), then each rewriting of the subject expression results in a new expression that is equal to the old subject expression. Since equality is transitive, any sequence of rewritings performed by a term-rewriting system results in an expression that is equal to the initial subject expression (the rewriting is *sound*). The rewritings terminate when there are no more redexes in the subject expression. If the rules are *confluent*, then the same initial subject expression always produces the same normal form (if it exists), regardless of the order in which the redexes are reduced (the system is *determinate*).

The differences between augmented term rewriting and standard term rewriting are all upwardly compatible extensions — a program written for a standard term-rewriting system will run and give the same answer on an augmented term-rewriting system. Consequently, for the set of programs that do not use any features specific to augmented term rewriting (such as local variables and binding), an augmented term-rewriting system will have the same desirable properties as a standard term-rewriting system (outlined in the preceding paragraph). In addition, since augmented term rewriting is more powerful than standard term rewriting, there are programs that have meaning to an augmented term-rewriting system, beyond those acceptable to a standard term-rewriting system. This section will mainly be concerned with the properties of these programs.

B.5.1 Expressiveness

As mentioned in chapter 3, some of our extensions to standard term rewriting, such as types and local variables, can be handled in the same semantic framework, and consequently retain the same properties as standard term rewriting. Indeed, types already exist in standard term-rewriting systems in the form of qualifiers on parameter variables.

Labels can be treated as an additional parameter in the head of rules, and local variables handled by preprocessing the rules to prepend the label name onto all local variables. For example, the rule

```
op1(Q) { op2(5, Q, x) }
```

can be preprocessed into two separate rules

```
Label : op1(Q) { op2(5, Q, Label . x) }
op1(Q) { op2(5, Q, newname . x) }
```

where *newname* generates unique names, and is only required to keep local variables in different instantiations of the same rule from having name conflicts with each other.

The major addition we are making to term rewriting is the `is` operator, which allows expressions to be bound to variable names. This operator is implemented using a higher-order rewrite rule that removes an equality constraint (an equation), replaces it with the Boolean truth value, and does an assignment to one of the variables in the equation. This newly bound variable will then be replaced by its value whenever it occurs elsewhere in the subject expression. This admits a limited form of nonlocal side effects to a term-rewriting system.

Adding binding increases the power and expressiveness of a term-rewriting system, so that, for example, simultaneous equations can be solved; but does it also affect determinacy? Intuitively, this addition seems reasonable. All we are doing is taking an equation, such as in the expression

```
x = 5 ; x
```

that is asserted to be true (by the semicolon), and saying that if x is 5, then we can replace x by 5 everywhere, and the expression will have the same meaning. Replacing x by 5, we get

```
5 = 5 ; 5
```

which can be further evaluated to

```
true ; 5
```

The semicolon allows us to remove its left argument and rewrite this expression to just the constant 5.

As in conventional languages, it is not the addition of binding that causes problems for the semantics of a language, it is the possibility of *multiple assignments*. Single-assignment languages, such as Lucid [Wadge 1985], allow a single value to be bound to a name, and retain a simple, nonprocedural semantics. In order to ensure that binding values to atoms does not give Bertrand any procedural semantics, we must guarantee that once a value is bound to a name that no other value can possibly be bound to it. Since a bound variable name is always immediately replaced by its value, this can never happen.

The addition of binding could affect termination, since binding a value to a name could cause the program to fail to terminate. For example, in the expression

```
x = x + 5 ; x
```

if the expression x + 5 is bound as the value of x, then x will be replaced by x + 5, and the x in x + 5 will be replaced by x + 5, and so on. The system will not be able to rewrite x because it will be trapped in an infinite loop. To prevent this from happening the rewrite rule for the is operator prohibits the value bound to a name from containing an instance of that name. In the example above, the equation is a contradiction, since no finite variable can be equal to 5 more than itself. If our augmented term-rewriting system used the standard library of rewrite rules for simplifying equations, this contradiction would have been detected by subtracting x from both sides of the equation, yielding

```
0 = 5 ; x
```

which can be read as "What is the value of x if 0 is equal to 5?"

B.5.2 Soundness

If the local variables of a rule were not prefixed by the (possibly generated) label name when the rule is instantiated, then local variables could affect soundness by introducing contradictions into an otherwise sound set of rules. For example, we saw in Section 3.2.2 how multiple invocations of the average rule with local variable mean introduced a contradiction into a conceptually valid set of constraints. By prefixing local variable names with the name of the (possibly generated by *newname*) label name, we guarantee that different invocations of the same rule will not try to "reuse" the same variable name, thus avoiding this problem, and preserving soundness.

In order for an augmented term rewriting to be considered sound, we must expand the conditions a set of rewrite rules must meet in order to be considered sound. Not only must the rules have equality as their similarity relation, as in a standard term-rewriting system, but the "rules" introduced by the is operator must also have equality as their similarity relation. Put another way, to be considered sound, each rule (in a program for an augmented term-rewriting system) must have equality as its similarity relation, and must only result in the binding of equals to equals. We can guarantee this by making sure that our rules only bind a value to a variable if the two were asserted to be equal by an equation. Assuming our rules meet this stronger notion of soundness, then the resulting normal form (if it exists) will be equal to the initial subject expression.

B.5.3 Confluence

For standard term rewriting, if a set of rules meets some simple restrictions (from Section 3.1) then an initial subject expression always reduces to the same normal form regardless of the order in which the redexes are reduced. For augmented term rewriting, confluence can possibly be affected by the "rules" introduced by the is operator. As for soundness, above, we expand the conditions that a set of rewrite rules must meet in order to be considered confluent. In particular, we require that the "rules" introduced by the is operator meet the same restrictions as other (normal) rules. For example, the rules introduced by the is operator must not overlap (see Section 3.1), or in other words, two different values may not be bound to the same variable. Fortunately, our existing restrictions on the is operator already ensure this.

   Even with the above restrictions, use of the is operator can still affect confluence. There are two possible ways in which this can occur. The first case is when the result returned might depend on the order in which a set of bindings is performed. For example, if we have the following subject expression:

```
x = exp1 ; y = exp2 ; f(x,y)
```

then we could bind exp1 as the value of x and then exp2 as the value of y, or we could do the bindings in the opposite order. If we bind x first, we are left with the expression

```
y = exp2 ; f(exp1,y)
```

If instead we bind y first, we are left with the expression

```
x = exp1 ; f(x,exp2)
```

Eventually we will perform the other binding, but if f(exp1,y) and f(x,exp2) could possibly rewrite to different final answers, then our system is not confluent. Fortunately, this cannot occur, which can easily be demonstrated by reducing this example to a simpler problem, with the subject expression f(x,y) and the same set of rewrite rules as before, but augmented by two additional rules:

```
x { exp1 }
y { exp2 }
```

Since rules added by the `is` operator must meet all of the restrictions for normal rules, this is perfectly legitimate. Our subject expression `f(x,y)` contains two redexes, so it will rewrite to either `f(exp1,y)` or `f(x,exp2)` depending on which redex is reduced first. We now have the same question of whether `f(exp1,y)` and `f(x,exp2)` could possibly rewrite to different final answers, but this problem does not use any features specific to augmented term rewriting. (It could be stated to a standard term-rewriting system, which we know is confluent). Therefore the original problem must be confluent (assuming the other rules meet our restrictions for confluence).

The second case that might affect confluence is where completely different bindings might occur. For example, in the subject expression

```
x = exp1 ; x = exp2 ; f(x)
```

the variable x can be given two different values depending on which binding is performed, resulting in one of the following two subject expressions:

```
exp1 = exp2 ; f(exp1)
exp2 = exp1 ; f(exp2)
```

Fortunately, regardless of which binding is made for the value of x, our term rewriting system is still required to prove that `exp1` is equal to `exp2`, so the answers returned will be equivalent. As discussed in Section B.5.2, in order for a set of rules to be considered sound they must result only in the binding of equals. If there are different equations in a subject expression that could give different bindings for the value of an atom, then that atom is equal to all those possible bindings (even though only one of them will ever be made). Consequently, if a set of rules is sound, then the different results that can be returned by an augmented term-rewriting system are all equivalent.

Unfortunately, for results that contain unbound variables, equivalent answers may still not be the same answer. Consider the subject expression

```
x = y ; x = z ; x
```

If we solve the leftmost equation first then the following bindings will be made:

```
x is y
y is z
```

The value of the subject expression (x) will be rewritten to y, and the y will be rewritten to z, and so z will be returned as the value of the expression. If, instead, we solve the second equation first, the bindings will be

```
x is z
z is y
```

and the value of the expression will be y. The normal form returned depends on the order in which bindings are performed. Of course, the variable x is certainly equal to both y and z, so either answer is correct, and neither answer is preferable to the other.

We will denote the set of possible values that can be returned by an augmented term-rewriting system (depending on the order of the bindings) by $\mathfrak{R}$. We are guaranteed that the elements of $\mathfrak{R}$ are all equal to each other. Furthermore, if the set $\mathfrak{R}$ contains a ground term (an expression containing no unbound variables), then that ground term will always be returned by the augmented term-rewriting system. This is a consequence of the fact that the is operator can only bind values to atoms, and not to constants.

For example, if we take the expression above and replace y by the constant 5, we get

```
x = 5 ; x = z ; x
```

The set $\mathfrak{R}$ contains x, z, and 5, but all sequences of bindings will produce the ground term. If the first equation is solved first, then 5 is bound to x, leaving

```
5 = z ; 5
```

The constant 5 is also bound to z, but z is unused. If the second equation is solved first, then z is bound as the value of x, leaving

```
z = 5 ; z
```

and the expression again simplifies to the constant 5. The second equation could also be solved by binding x to z, but since z is unused in the rest of the expression, this reduces to the first case, above. If an expression can possibly be reduced to a ground term, then that term will always be returned regardless of the order of the bindings.

Consequently, an augmented term-rewriting system is **ground confluent**, that is, confluent for answers that are ground terms. If our conditions on rules are met, then an augmented term-rewriting system will always produce the same result regardless of the order in which the redexes are reduced, for results that do not contain any unbound atoms. If all potential results contain some unbound atoms, then different normal forms may be produced depending on the order of evaluation, but these different normal forms are all equivalent (assuming the rules are sound). This is actually a stronger statement than can be made for standard term-rewriting systems since they do not have bindable atoms.

An Interpreter

This appendix presents a working interpreter for an augmented term rewriting system written in Scheme (Scheme has been described as a lexically scoped dialect of LISP [Rees 1986]). In addition, we have restricted ourselves to a purely functional subset of Scheme, so this program will also serve as an executable semantics for augmented term rewriting. Scheme is an especially appropriate language for this task because of its clear and simple semantics.

This interpreter does run, and has been tested on a variety of inputs, but it is not meant to be used as a production interpreter since it was written for clarity rather than speed. The major purpose of this program is to codify precisely the semantics presented in Appendix B. It could be used as the basis for a faster interpreter, however, or to verify the behavior of a production interpreter.

There are three differences between the following program (which I will call the *executable semantics*) and the semantics presented in Appendix B (the *operational semantics*). Only the first one is significant. In the operational semantics, if the subject expression contained more than one redex, the order in which they were reduced was not defined. In the following executable semantics, the outermost redex is reduced first. If there is more than one outermost redex, the leftmost is reduced first. Since the order of reduction does not matter this should not cause any problems. Strictly speaking, however, a semantics should not restrict the order in which the reductions are performed (for example, the executable semantics could find all possible redexes, and then randomly choose one of them).

The second difference is purely syntactic and could be handled by a simple preprocessing step. The syntax of the input language accepted by the executable semantics differs from the syntax used by the operational semantics (which, in turn, differs from the syntax actually used by Bertrand). In this syntax, expressions are constructed from Scheme lists. These lists all begin with a symbol that indicates what kind of expression the list represents. Table C.1 presents the correspondence between the two different syntaxes.

Table C.1		
Expression Type	Operational	Executable
variable	`name`	`('var name)`
compound variable	`n1.n2.n3`	`('var n1 n2 n3)`
parameter	`pname`	`('parameter pname)`
compound variable with first element a parameter	`p1.n2.n3`	`('parameter p1 n2 n3)`
parameter (with guard)	`pname'type`	`('typed pname type)`
parameter (multiple guards)	`–N/A–`	`('typed name t1 t2 t3)`
numeric constant	`123`	`('constant . 123)`
term	`op(args)`	`('term (:) op args)`
labeled term	`label: op(arg)`	`('term (label) op arg)`
compound labeled term	`l1.l2: op(arg)`	`('term (l1 l2) op arg)`
"is" expression	`is(expr1, expr2)`	`('is expr1 expr2)`

In this syntax, all terms (operators) must have a label. If a term is to be unlabeled it is given a label consisting of a list containing a single colon (which will be replaced by a generated label during execution).

We define a number of help functions for detecting the different kinds of expressions:

```
(define constant? (lambda (x) (and (pair? x)
                                   (eq? (car x) 'constant))))
(define parameter? (lambda (x) (and (pair? x)
                                    (eq? (car x) 'parameter))))
(define typed? (lambda (x) (and (pair? x) (eq? (car x) 'typed))))
(define var? (lambda (x) (and (pair? x) (eq? (car x) 'var))))
(define term? (lambda (x) (and (pair? x) (eq? (car x) 'term))))
(define isis? (lambda (x) (and (pair? x) (eq? (car x) 'is))))
```

The last difference between the executable semantics and the operational semantics can also be handled by a preprocessing step. The executable semantics does not allow types to have supertypes. Instead, it allows a guard on a parameter variable in the head of a rule to have multiple guard types. Since the supertype relation is a strict hierarchy, any type can only have a finite number of supertypes. Thus if we use a preprocessor to replace all guards by a list containing the transitive closure of the supertype relation for that guard, the following executable semantics (without supertypes) is equivalent to the operational semantics. For example, if $\tau 1$ is a supertype of $\tau 2$, and $\tau 2$ is a supertype of $\tau 3$, then a guard on a parameter that contains the type $\tau 3$ would be replaced by the list $(\tau 3\ \tau 2\ \tau 1)$.

Our program uses two data types (rule and state), both represented as vectors. A **rule** is a vector containing a head expression, a body expression, and an optional tag. These three elements of a rule are accessed using the functions head, body, and tag. If a rule does not contain a tag, then #f (the Scheme constant representing the boolean value FALSE) is returned instead.

```
(define head (lambda (x) (vector-ref x 0)))   ; head of rule
(define body (lambda (x) (vector-ref x 1)))   ; body of rule
(define tag                                   ; tag of rule
   (lambda (x)
      (if (=? (vector-length x) 3)
          (vector-ref x 2)
          #f)))        ; return false if no tag
```

A **state** is a four-tuple, containing a subject expression, a global name space, a global type space, and an integer. The integer is used for generating label names for unlabeled redexes (the *newname* function from Sections 3.2.2 and B.2.2). The elements of a state are accessed using the functions subject, globals, typesp, and newname.

```
(define make-state (lambda (s g t n) (vector s g t n)))
(define subject (lambda (x) (vector-ref x 0)))
(define globals (lambda (x) (vector-ref x 1)))
(define typesp (lambda (x) (vector-ref x 2)))
(define newname (lambda (x) (vector-ref x 3)))
```

We also define four functions that take a state and return a new state with one of the elements updated.

```
(define replace-s           ; replace subject expression in state
   (lambda (state new-subject)
      (vector new-subject
              (globals state)
              (typesp state)
              (newname state))))

(define replace-g           ; replace globals in state
   (lambda (state new-globals)
      (vector (subject state)
              new-globals
              (typesp state)
              (newname state))))
```

```
(define replace-t              ; replace type space in state
   (lambda (state new-typesp)
      (vector (subject state)
              (globals state)
              new-typesp
              (newname state))))

(define incr-n                 ; increment label generator in state
   (lambda (state)
      (vector (subject state)
              (globals state)
              (typesp state)
              (+ 1 (newname state)))))
```

The main function of the augmented term rewriter takes a subject expression and a list of rules, constructs a state, and passes the initial state and the rules to the rewriter.

```
(define augmented-term-rewriter
   (lambda (subject-exp rules)
      (rewrite
       (make-state              ; state
        subject-exp               ; subject expression
        init-phi                  ; initial global name space
        init-phi                  ; initial type space
        0)                        ; initial generated label name
       rules)))                 ; rules

(define init-phi '((*reserved* . *reserved*)))
```

This function returns a state, which was returned by the function `rewrite`. Name spaces (and type spaces) are represented as a list of name–value pairs. The variable `init-phi` represents the empty name space.

The function `rewrite` takes a state and a list of rules, and returns a new state containing the completely rewritten subject expression, a global name space containing all of the bound variables and their values, a type space containing all the typed variables and their types, and an integer that indicates how many label names were generated:

```
(define rewrite
   (lambda (state rules)
      (let ((no-bv-state (rewrite-globals state)))
           (if no-bv-state                      ; bound var was found
               (rewrite no-bv-state rules)
               (let ((new-state (rewrite-exp state rules rules)))
                    (if new-state               ; match (or "is") found
                        (rewrite new-state rules)
                        state)))))))
```

Rewrite first calls the function `rewrite-globals` which replaces bound variables by their value (corresponding to the "rule" Γ). If a bound variable was found, `rewrite-globals` returns a new state, otherwise it returns #f. If a bound variable was found, then `rewrite` calls itself recursively. Otherwise, `rewrite-exp` is called, which rewrites subexpressions of the subject expression that match one of the rules, and also rewrites `is` expressions (corresponding to the "rule" Λ). The reason for having a separate rewriter for bound variables, rather than combining it into `rewrite-exp`, is because of the requirement that all bound variables be replaced by their values before any more binding is performed. If no redexes are found by either `rewrite-globals` or `rewrite-exp` (they both return #f) then `rewrite` terminates and returns the state.

Rewrite-exp is passed two copies of the rules. It first attempts to match the outermost term of the subject expression against the first rule in rules (by calling `try-rule`). If this fails, it recursively calls itself, removing the head of the list of rules:

```
(define rewrite-exp
   (lambda (state rules-left-to-try rules)
      (if (null? rules-left-to-try)
          (rewrite-subexpressions state rules)
          (let ((new-state (try-rule
                               state
                               (car rules-left-to-try))))
               (if new-state
                   new-state
                   (rewrite-exp state
                                (cdr rules-left-to-try)
                                rules)))))))
```

When the list of rules is empty, then the outermost term has failed to match any rule in rules, so `rewrite-subexpressions` is called with the original list of rules.

```
(define rewrite-subexpressions
   (lambda (state rules)
      (let ((expr (subject state)))
           (cond ((constant? expr) #f)
                 ((var? expr) #f)
                 ((term? expr)
                  (rewrite-args (first3 expr)
                                (cdddr expr)
                                state
                                rules))
                 ((isis? expr) (rewrite-is state))
                 (else (error "Invalid subject expression:"
                              expr))))))

(define rewrite-args
   (lambda (previous-terms terms-to-try state rules)
      (if (null? terms-to-try)
          #f
          (let ((new-state (rewrite-exp
                              (replace-s state (car terms-to-try))
                              rules rules)))
              (if new-state
                  (replace-s
                    new-state
                    (append previous-terms
                            (cons (subject new-state)
                                  (cdr terms-to-try))))
                  (rewrite-args
                    (append previous-terms
                            (list (car terms-to-try)))
                    (cdr terms-to-try) state rules))))))

(define first3    ; return the first 3 elements of a list
   (lambda (alist)
      (list (car alist) (cadr alist) (caddr alist))))
```

If the outermost term is an operator with arguments, then `rewrite` is called recursively on each of the arguments (by `rewrite-args`). If any argument was a redex, then that transformed argument is reinserted into the subject expression in the state. The `first3` function is used to skip over the first three elements of a list representing an expression (the symbol ′term, the label, and the operator) when calling `rewrite-args`.

If the outermost term is an `is` expression (it matches the "rule" Λ), then `rewrite-subexpressions` calls the function `rewrite-is`:

```
(define rewrite-is
   (lambda (state)
      (let ((expr (subject state))
            (space (globals state)))
         (if (and (pair? (cdr expr))          ; two args?
                  (var? (cadr expr))          ; first is var?
                  (pair? (cddr expr))         ; second is expr?
                  (not (lookup (cdadr expr)
                               space))        ; var not bound?
                  (not (rewrite-globals       ; var not in expr?
                        (make-state (caddr expr)
                                    (bind (cdadr expr)
                                          '()
                                          init-phi)
                              init-phi 0))))
            (replace-g (replace-s state true-expr)
                  (bind (cdadr expr) (caddr expr) space))
            (error "invalid "is" expression:" expr)))))))
```

```
(define true-expr '(expr (:) true))
```

`Rewrite-is` checks to make sure the `is` expression is well formed, that the variable is not already bound, and that the value does not contain an instance of the variable. If everything is in order, then a new state with a new subject expression and a new global name space is returned. The new global name space is the old global name space with the addition of a new name/value pair for the new bound variable. The new subject expression is the nullary operator (constant) `true`.

The `try-rule` function (which was called by `rewrite-exp`) takes a state and a single rule, and tries to match the head of the rule against the subject expression in the state.

```
(define try-rule
    (lambda (state rule)
       (let ((phi (match state (head rule) init-phi)))
            (if phi
                (let ((label (get-label (subject state)
                                        (newname state))))
                    (replace-s
                     (bind-type
                      (if (eq? (last label) (newname state))
                          (incr-n state)
                          state)
                       rule label)
                     (transform (body rule) phi label)))
                #f)))))
```

Match returns #f if there is no match, otherwise it returns a name space that gives
the bindings for all the parameter variables in the head of the rule. If a match was
found then get-label returns the label of the matched subexpression, or generates
a label. Try-rule returns a new state, with a new subject expression, possibly a new
type space (if the rule was typed), and possibly an incremented newname (if the label
was generated). The new subject expression is the transformed body of the rule.

Match takes a state (containing a subject expression) a pattern (head of a rule)
and an initial parameter name space, and builds the parameter name space.

```
(define match
    (lambda (state pattern phi)
       (let ((expr (subject state)))
            (cond
              ((parameter? pattern) (bind (cadr pattern) expr phi))
              ((and (typed? pattern) (var? expr))
               (let ((var-type (lookup (cdr expr) (typesp state))))
                   (if (and var-type
                            (memq var-type (cddr pattern)))
                       (bind (cadr pattern) expr phi)
                       #f)))
              ((and (typed? pattern) (constant? expr)
                    (eq? (caddr pattern) 'constant))
               (bind (cadr pattern) expr phi))
              ((and (constant? pattern) (constant? expr)
                    (=? (cdr pattern) (cdr expr))) phi)
              ((and (term? pattern) (term? expr)
                    (eq? (caddr pattern) (caddr expr)))
               (match-args (replace-s state (cdddr expr))
                           (cdddr pattern) phi))
```

```
         ((var? pattern)
          (error "Local variable in head of rule"))
         (else #f)))))

(define match-args
   (lambda (state patterns phi)
      (let ((args (subject state)))
         (cond
          ((and (null? args) (null? patterns)) phi)
          ((null? args) #f)
          ((null? patterns) #f)
          (else
             (let ((new-phi (match (replace-s state (car args))
                                    (car patterns) phi)))
                 (if new-phi
                     (match-args (replace-s state (cdr args))
                                  (cdr patterns) new-phi)
                     #f)))))))
```

`Get-label` checks to see if the last element of the label of the matched expression is a colon, and if so replaces it with a generated name, which is simply a number (the user is not allowed to use numbers for labels, so there can be no conflict from generated labels):

```
(define get-label
   (lambda (expr lgen)
      (if (eq? (last (cadr expr)) ':)
          (replace-last (cadr expr) lgen)
          (cadr expr))))

(define last        ; return the last element of a proper list
   (lambda (lst)
      (if (pair? lst)
          (if (null? (cdr lst))
              (car lst)
              (last (cdr lst)))
          (error "Cannot return last element of atom:" lst))))

(define replace-last  ; replace the last element of a list
   (lambda (lst val)
      (if (and (pair? lst) (null? (cdr lst)))
          (list val)
          (cons (car lst) (replace-last (cdr lst) val)))))
```

Bind-type (**called by** try-rule **if a match was found) binds a type to the label in the type space if the rule was tagged (even if the label was generated):**

```
(define bind-type
   (lambda (state rule label)
      (let ((rule-tag (tag rule)))
         (if rule-tag
            (replace-t state
                        (bind label rule-tag (typesp state)))
            state)))))
```

The function transform **takes the body of the matched rule, a parameter name space, and a label, and returns a transformed expression:**

```
(define transform
   (lambda (rule-body phi label)
      (cond
         ((parameter? rule-body)
          (let ((param-val (lookup (cadr rule-body) phi)))
             (if param-val
                 (if (=? (length (cdr rule-body)) 1)
                     param-val        ; not qualified parameter
                     (if (var? param-val)
                         (cons (car param-val)
                               (append (cdr param-val)
                                       (cddr rule-body)))
                         (error
                          "A qualified parameter "
                          "matched a non-variable:"
                          param-val)))
                 (error "Parameter in body that is not in head:"
                        rule-body))))
         ((var? rule-body)
          (cons (car rule-body) (append label (cdr rule-body)))))
         ((constant? rule-body) rule-body)
         ((term? rule-body)
          (append (list
                   (car rule-body)                      ; 'term
                   (append label (cadr rule-body))
                   (caddr rule-body))
                  (transform-args (cdddr rule-body) phi label)))
         ((isis? rule-body)
          (cons (car rule-body)
                (transform-args (cdr rule-body) phi label)))
         (else (error "Invalid body of rule:" rule-body)))))
```

```
(define transform-args
   (lambda (args phi label)
      (if (null? args)
          '()
          (cons (transform (car args) phi label)
                (transform-args (cdr args) phi label)))))
```

We still need to define the functions for dealing with name spaces (including parameter and global name spaces, and type spaces).

```
(define bind
   (lambda (var val name-space)
      (cons (cons var val) name-space)))

(define lookup
   (lambda (var name-space)
      (let ((entry (assoc var name-space)))
         (if entry
             (cdr entry)
             #f))))
```

Bind constructs a name–value pair, and adds it onto the beginning of the name space list. Lookup searches the list for the specified name. They are quite simple (and, of course, quite inefficient).

Now that we have finished with rewrite-exp we can define rewrite-globals, which replaces bound variables by their values.

```
(define rewrite-globals
   (lambda (state)
      (let ((expr (subject state))
            (space (globals state)))
         (cond
          ((var? expr)
           (let ((val (lookup (cdr expr) (globals state))))
              (if val  ; variable is bound
                  (replace-s state val)  ; replace by value
                  #f)))
          ((constant? expr) #f)
          ((term? expr)
           (rewrite-g-args (first3 expr) (cdddr expr) state))
          ((isis? expr)
           (rewrite-g-args (list (car expr)) (cdr expr) state))
          (else (error "invalid subject expression:" expr))))))
```

```
(define rewrite-g-args
    (lambda (previous-terms terms state)
       (if (null? terms)
           #f
           (let ((new-state (rewrite-globals
                                (replace-s state (car terms)))))
                 (if new-state
                     (replace-s new-state
                         (append previous-terms
                                 (cons (subject new-state)
                                       (cdr terms))))
                     (rewrite-g-args
                      (append previous-terms (list (car terms)))
                      (cdr terms) state))))))
```

The main purpose of this executable semantics is to precisely state what augmented term rewriting does, and how it does it. It can also be used to validate implementations of augmented term-rewriting systems. As an actual augmented term-rewriting system, however, it would be extremely inefficient. It also has no primitives (such as addition), or the primitives to detect the interestingness of atoms that would need to be added to make a usable system.

References

Abelson, H., and Sussman, G. J., 1985. *Structure and Interpretation of Computer Programs.* MIT press, Cambridge, Mass.

Ackerman, W. B., February 1982 "Data Flow Languages," *IEEE Computer* 15(2), 15-25.

Aho, A., and Corasick, M., June 1975. "Efficient String Matching: an Aid to Bibliographic Search," *Communications of the ACM* 18(6), 333-343.

Aho, A., and Ganapathi, M., 1985. "Efficient Tree Pattern Matching: an Aid to Code Generation," 12th ACM Symposium on Principles of Programming Languages.

Ashcroft, E., and Wadge, W., July 1977. "Lucid, a Nonprocedural Language with Iteration," *Communications of the ACM* 20(7), 519-526.

Backus, J., August 1978. "Can Programming be Liberated from the von Neumann Style? A Functional Style and its Algebra of Programs," *Communications of the ACM* 21:8, 613-641.

Blaauw, G. A., and Brooks, F. P., (in press). *Computer Architecture,* Addison–Wesley, Reading, Mass.

Borning, A., July 1979. *ThingLab — A Constraint-Oriented Simulation Laboratory,* Xerox PARC technical report SSL-79-3, Palo Alto, Calif. [This is a revised version of Borning's Ph.D. thesis, also published as Stanford technical report STAN-CS-79-746.]

Borning, A., October 1981. "The Programming Language Aspects of ThingLab, A Constraint-Oriented Simulation Laboratory," *ACM Transactions on Programming Languages and Systems* 3(4), 353-387.

Borning, A., September 1985a. *Constraints and Functional Programming,* University of Washington Computer Science Department Technical Report No. 85-09-05, Seattle, Wash.

Borning, A., September 1985b. *Defining Constraints Graphically,* University of Washington Computer Science Department Technical Report No. 85-09-06, Seattle, Wash.

Buchanan, B. G., Shortliffe, E. H., October 1984. *Rule-Based Expert Systems,* Addison–Wesley, Reading, Mass. [The MYCIN experiments of the Stanford Heuristic Programming Project.]

Bundy, A., 1983. *The Computer Modeling of Mathematical Reasoning*, Academic Press, London. [Term rewriting and graph transformation.]

Clocksin, W., Mellish, C., 1981. *Programming in Prolog*, Springer-Verlag, New York.

Curry, H. B., and Feys, R., 1958. *Combinatory Logic Volume 1*, North-Holland, Amsterdam.

Derman, E., and Van Wyk, C. J., December 1984. 8("A Simple Equation Solver and Its Application to Financial Modeling," *Software – Practice and Experience* 14(12), 1169-1181. [This equation solver is similar to the one used as the constraint satisfier in Van Wyk's language IDEAL.]

Dershowitz, N., and Plaisted, D. A., July 1985. "Logic Programming *cum* Applicative Programming," 1985 Symposium on Logic Programming, 54-66. [Using narrowing as an operational semantics for logic programming.]

Doyle, J., 1977. *Truth Maintenance Systems for Problem Solving*, M.S. thesis, MIT, Cambridge, Mass.

Duisberg, R., August 1986. *Constraint-Based Animation: Temporal Constraints in the Animus System*, Ph.D. Thesis, University of Washington Technical Report 86-09-01 (Ph.D. thesis), Seattle, Wash. [also Tektronix Technical Report CR-86-37.]

Fixx, J. F., 1972. *Games for the Superintelligent*, Doubleday, New York.

Goguen, J. A., and Meseguer, J., August 1984. "Equality, Types, Modules, and (Why Not?) Generics for Logic Programming," *Journal of Logic Programming* 1(2), 179-210. [EQLOG is a logic programming language that can do constraint satisfaction.]

Goldberg, A., and Robson, D., 1983. *Smalltalk-80: The Language and Its Implementation*, Addison-Wesley, Menlo Park, Calif.

Gosling, J., May 1983. *Algebraic Constraints*, CMU Technical Report CS-83-132 (Ph.D. thesis), Carnegie–Mellon University, Pittsburg.

Gosling, J., 1980. "The Mumble Microcode Compiler," *The Cm* Multiprocessor Project: A Research Review*, Carnegie-Mellon University Computer Science Department, Pittsburg. [Code optimization as a constraint satisfaction problem.]

Hoffmann, C. M., and O'Donnell, M., January 1982. "Programming with Equations," *ACM*Transactions 4(1), 83-112. [Term rewriting.]

Hoffmann, C. M., O'Donnell, M. J., and Strandh, R. I., December 1985. "Implementation of an Interpreter for Abstract Equations," *Software — Practice and Experience* 15(12), 1185-1204. [Fast algorithm for term rewriting.]

Hullot, J-M., 1980. "Canonical Forms and Unification," *Proceedings of the 5th Workshop on Automated Deduction*, Springer-Verlag Lecture Notes, New York, 318-334. [Discussion of narrowing.]

International Standards Organization, May 1981. "Graphical Kernel System (GKS), Version 6.6," ISO, Geneva, Switzerland.

Jayaraman, B., and Silbermann F., August 1986. "Equations, Sets, and Reduction Semantics for Functional and Logic Programming," ACM LISP and Functional Programming Conference, 320-331.

Johnson, T., 1963. "Sketchpad III, A Computer Program for Drawing in Three Dimensions," IFIPS Proceedings of the Spring Joint Computer Conference. [An extension to Sketchpad to allow it to construct three dimensional objects.]

Kaehler, C., 1983. "MacPaint Manual", Apple Computer, Cupertino, Calif.

Kernighan, B. W., March 1982. *PIC — A Graphics Language for Typesetting, User Manual,* Bell Labs Computer Science Technical Report No. 85.

Knuth, D. E., 1979. *TeX and METAFONT, New Directions in Typesetting,* published jointly by the American Mathematical Society and Digital Press.

Konopasek, M., and Jayaraman, S., 1984. *The TK!Solver Book,* Osborne/McGraw-Hill, Berkeley, Calif.

Kowalski, R. A., August 1979. "Algorithm = Logic + Control," *Communications of the ACM* 22(7), 424-431.

Leler, W., August 1983. "A Small, High-Speed Data-Flow Processor," *Proceedings of the International Conference on Parallel Processing,* 341-343.

Leler, W., May 1984. *Named Data Types for Pattern Matching Languages,* Tektronix Computer Research Lab technical report.

Leler, W., June 1985. "Constraint Languages for Computer Aided Design," *SIGDA Newsletter* 15(2), 11-15.

Levitt, D., Spring 1984. *Machine Tongues X: Constraint Languages, Computer Music Journal* 8(1), 9-21. [Introduction to TK!Solver, plus author's jazz composition system.]

MathLab, January 1983. *MACSYMA Reference Manual,* The MathLab Group, Laboratory for Computer Science, MIT, Cambridge, Mass.

Mellish, C. S., 1980. *An Alternative to Structure-Sharing in the Implementation of a Prolog Interpreter*, Department of Artificial Intelligence Research Paper 150, University of Edinburgh, Scotland.

Nelson, G., January 1984. *How to use Juno*, Manuscript CGN11, Computer Science Laboratory, Xerox PARC, Palo Alto, Calif. [Juno introduced automatic programming to a constraint language.]

Nelson, G., July 1985. "JUNO, a Constraint-Based Graphics System" *SIGGRAPH Computer Graphics* 19(3), 235-243.

Newell, A., and Simon, H. A., 1963. "GPS, A Program that Simulates Human Thought," in Feigenbaum, E. A., and Feldman, J., *Computers and Thought*, McGraw-Hill, New York, 279-293. [The General Problem Solver.]

Nydegger, R., Fall 1973. Lectures for Psychology 201a – Introduction to Psychology, Rice University, Houston.

O'Donnell, M. J., 1977. *Computing in Systems Described by Equations, Lecture Notes in Computer Science 58*, Springer-Verlag, New York. [Formal treatment of term rewriting.]

O'Donnell, M. J., 1985. *Equational Logic as a Programming Language*, The MIT Press, Cambridge, Mass. [The Purdue Equational Interpreter.]

Pavlidis, T., and Van Wyk, C. J., July 1985. "An Automatic Beautifier for Drawings and Illustrations," *SIGGRAPH Computer Graphics* 19(3), 225-234.

Rees, J., Clinger, W., ed., December 1986. "The Revised^3 Report on the Algorithmic Language Scheme," *ACM SIGPLAN Notices* 21(12), 37-79.

Skedzielewski, S., and Glauert, J., June 1984. *IF1, An Intermediate Form for Applicative Languages*, Lawrence Livermore Labs Technical Report, Livermore, Calif.

Steele, G. L., August 1980. *The Definition and Implementation of a Computer Programming Language Based on Constraints*, MIT AI-TR.595 (Ph.D. thesis), Cambridge, Mass.

Steele, G. L., and Sussman, G. J., June 1979. "CONSTRAINTS," APL conference proceedings part 1, APL Quote Quad, 208-225.

Sutherland, I., January 1963. "SKETCHPAD: A Man–Machine Graphical Communication System," IFIPS Proceedings of the Spring Joint Computer Conference. [see also his Ph.D. thesis from MIT.]

Treleaven, P., Brownbridge, D. and Hopkins, R., March 1982. "Data-Driven and Demand-Driven Computer Architectures," *Computing Surveys* 14(1), 93-143.

Turner, D., October 1981. "The Semantic Elegance of Applicative Languages," *ACM Proceedings of the Conference on Functional Programming Languages and Computer Architecture.* [SASL and KRC are applicative languages, but have some similarities to constraint languages.]

Van Wyk, C. J., June 1980. *A Language for Typesetting Graphics,* Ph.D. thesis, Stanford University, Palo Alto, Calif. [IDEAL.]

Van Wyk, C. J., December 1981. "IDEAL User's Manual," Bell Labs Computer Science Technical Report 103, Murray Hill, New Jersey.

Van Wyk, C. J., April 1982. "A High-Level Language for Specifying Pictures," *ACM Transactions on Graphics* 1(2), 163-182.

Wadge, W., and Ashcroft, E., 1985. *Lucid, the Data-Flow Programming Language,* Academic Press, New York.

Winkler, F., Buchberger, B., Lichtenberger, F., Rolletschek, March 1985. "An Algorithm for Constructing Canonical Bases of Polynomial Ideals," *ACM Transactions on Mathematical Software* 11(1), 66-78. [Groebner basis.]

Index